COURSE **3** **McDougal Littell Middle School**

Math

Larson   Boswell   Kanold   Stiff

Special Activities Book

The Special Activities Book contains a wide variety of
classroom activities. These include activities for the
start of the school year, activities for substitute teachers,
activities for use before school holidays, and short
change-of-pace activities.

McDougal Littell
A HOUGHTON MIFFLIN COMPANY

Evanston, Illinois   •   Boston   •   Dallas

ISBN: 0-618-28038-3

23456789–BHV–07 06 05 04 03

Contents

Contents

Start of School Activities   These activities are designed to be used in class at the beginning of the school year. The activities involve the mathematics learned during the previous year, thus giving students a subtle review of concepts that they learned in earlier grades. Some activities are designed for individual work; others are group activities.

Mathematical Activities for Substitutes   These activities are designed to be used in class by a substitute teacher, instead of the substitute teaching a new lesson. The activities are a mixture of fun practice and review, math games, and group activities, and they should take most of the class period. There are two activities for each chapter.

Activities for Days Before Holidays   These activities are designed to be used in class before the major school vacations—Thanksgiving, the December vacation, winter vacation, and spring vacation. The activities cover only the mathematics that students have learned up to that point in the school year. The activities are a mixture of fun practice and review, math games, and group activities. There are two activities from which to choose for each vacation period.

Change of Pace Activities   These are short activities that can be completed in class in about ten to twenty minutes. These activities can be used for the transition times in a class period, such as the last few minutes of class after instruction has concluded, the second half of class after a quiz, or the remainder of a block-scheduling period after a test. The activities are a mixture of fun practice and review, math games, and group activities. There is one activity for every other lesson, and the activity applies to the math taught in the previous two lessons.

Make the Numbers

Use at the beginning of the school year.

Rearrange the 6 digits and a decimal point to make each number. Use each digit once. Place the decimal point in any part of the number. For numbers less than 1, a zero before the decimal point is not required.

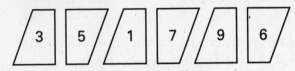

1. the greatest possible number _____
2. the least possible number _____
3. the number nearest to 40 _____
4. the number nearest to 500 _____
5. the number nearest to $\frac{8}{10}$ _____
6. the number nearest to $\frac{38}{100}$ _____
7. the least number that is greater than 6350 _____
8. the greatest number that is less than 678 _____
9. the number nearest to $\frac{651}{1000}$ _____
10. the number nearest to fifty-seven hundredths _____
11. the number nearest to nine and seventy-four hundredths _____
12. the number nearest to three and one hundred fifty-eight thousandths _____

Name _____ Date _____

Consecutive Integers

Use at the beginning of the school year.

Consecutive integers are integers in counting order. For example, -18, -17, and -16 are three consecutive integers. Consecutive even integers are two apart; so are consecutive odd integers.

You can write and solve an equation to find consecutive integers. Study these two examples.

Find three consecutive integers whose sum is -18. *Think:* Use a variable.

Let n = the least integer.

$$n + (n + 1) + (n + 2) = -18$$
$$3n + 3 = -18$$
$$3n = -21$$
$$n = -7$$

The integers are -7, -6, and -5.

Find three consecutive *even* integers whose sum is -24. *Think:* The integers are 2 apart.

Let n = the least integer.

$$n + (n + 2) + (n + 4) = -24$$
$$3n + 6 = -24$$
$$3n = -30$$
$$n = -10$$

The integers are -10, -8, and -6.

Read each problem carefully. Choose a variable and then write and solve an equation. Check to see that your solution works.

1. Find two consecutive integers whose sum is -25. _____

2. Find three consecutive integers whose sum is 72. _____

3. Find three consecutive integers whose sum is -33. _____

4. Find two consecutive even integers whose sum is -46. _____

5. Find three consecutive even integers whose sum is -90. _____

6. Find four consecutive integers whose sum is 78. _____

7. Find three consecutive odd integers whose sum is -87. _____

8. Find five consecutive integers whose sum is 0. _____

Use the Properties

Use at the beginning of the school year.

For each expression, use the property named to write an equivalent expression.

Expression	Property	Equivalent Expression
1. $6 + 12$	Commutative	_____
2. $3(3 + 7)$	Commutative	_____
3. $6(n + 5)$	Distributive	_____
4. $x + 3$	Commutative	_____
5. $(n + 4) + 6$	Associative	_____
6. $3(y + 12)$	Distributive	_____
7. $2(5 \cdot n)$	Associative	_____
8. $9x + 5$	Commutative	_____

Identify the property used to form the second expression from the first expression.

First Expression	Second Expression	Name of Property
9. $(3n + 6) - 2n - 4 \rightarrow$	$3n + (6 - 2n) - 4$	_____
10. $3n + (6 - 2n) - 4 \rightarrow$	$3n + (-2n + 6) - 4$	_____
11. $3n - 2n + 6 - 4 \rightarrow$	$(3 - 2)n + 6 - 4$	_____
12. $3n + 6 - 2n - 4 \rightarrow$	$3(n + 2) - 2(n + 2)$	_____
13. $(3n) \cdot 4 + 8 \rightarrow$	$3(n \cdot 4) + 8$	_____
14. $3(n \cdot 4) + 8 \rightarrow$	$3(4n) + 8$	_____
15. $4(3n) + 4(8) \rightarrow$	$4(3n + 8)$	_____

16. Count the number of times you used each property in Exercises 9–15 above. Write each count above the property name below to find the greatest prime number between 14^2 and 15^2.

_____   _____   _____

Commutative   Associative   Distributive

Crack the Code

Use at the beginning of the school year.

Circle the expression in each row whose value is different from the others.

1. **T.** 4^3 **E.** 3^4 **R.** 8^2
2. **P.** 4^2 **N.** $2^3 + 8$ **M.** 2^8
3. **S.** 2^5 **P.** $4^2 + 4^2$ **A.** 4^4
4. **A.** 3^3 **O.** $3 + 3 + 3$ **N.** $3^2 + 18$
5. **W.** $10^2 - 5^2$ **D.** 125   **K.** 5^3
6. **J.** 10,000   **W.** 100^3 **C.** 10^4
7. **D.** 9.5×10^2 **M.** 95×10 **N.** 9500
8. **P.** 3^5 **L.** 5^3 **H.** 243
9. **R.** 256^{10} **A.** 40^4 **E.** 2,560,000

Use your answers to Exercises 1–9 to answer the question. Write the letter matching each correct answer in the space above the exercise number.

Question: It took this 1830 invention nearly fifty years to gain some popularity. Then, when gasoline engines were added to it in 1919, every homeowner wanted one. This time-saving machine was here to stay. What is it?

Answer: A ____ ____ ____ ____ ____ ____ ____ ____ ____ .

          8   3   6   7   2   4   5   1   9

Name _____ Date _____

Form the Fractions

Use at the beginning of the school year.

Solve each equivalent fraction problem. You will need to use at least one number more than once in order to write the fractions.

1. Use the numbers 2, 6, and 18 to write two fractions equivalent to $\frac{1}{3}$.

_____

2. Use the numbers 1, 25, and 5 to write two fractions equivalent to 0.2.

_____

3. Use the numbers 12, 6, and 3 to write two fractions equivalent to 0.5.

_____

4. Use the numbers 9, 16, and 12 to write two fractions equivalent to seventy-five hundredths.

_____

5. Use the numbers 2 and 8 and one other integer to write two fractions equivalent to $\frac{1}{4}$.

_____

6. Use the numbers 3 and 15 and one other integer to write two fractions equivalent to 0.2.

_____

7. Use the number 4 and two other integers to write two fractions equivalent to $66\frac{2}{3}\%$.

_____

8. *Challenge*   Make up an equivalent fractions problem similar to those above. Solve it yourself first. Then trade with a classmate.

_____

Name _____ Date _____

Parts of a Whole
Use at the beginning of the school year.

The large rectangle represents one whole. Section $A = \frac{1}{3}$.

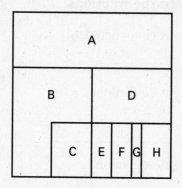

Study the picture above. Then solve the problems.

1. $A + D =$ _____

2. $C + D =$ _____

3. $E + F =$ _____

4. $A \times B =$ _____

5. $A - B =$ _____

6. $(E + F) - H =$ _____

7. $(A + D) - C =$ _____

8. $(C + E + F) - D =$ _____

9. $(B + D) \times (E + F) =$ _____

10. $B - (G + F) =$ _____

11. $A \div C =$ _____

12. $(A + D) \div B =$ _____

Name _____   Date _____

Crossnumber Puzzle

Use at the beginning of the school year.

Find the answer to each problem in the Across and Down columns. Then fill in the answer in the appropriate spaces on the puzzle.

Across

1. $\frac{1}{8} = 0.$_____

4. $\frac{2}{5} =$ _____ %

6. $0.1 =$ _____ %

7. $\frac{41}{50} =$ _____ %

9. $\frac{5}{8}$ of 1000 = _____

11. $\frac{45}{1000} = 0.$ _____

12. 20% of 50 = _____

14. 225% of 100 = _____

16. mean of 22, 31, 20, 39

17. 0.7% = 0. _____

20. 87.5% of 1000 = _____

22. mode of 16, 42, 5, 42, 80, 8

24. 35 : 140 = _____ : 420

25. _____ : 1000 = 3.75 : 10

26. 1.5 : 1 = _____ : 100

Down

2. 0.26 = _____ %

3. $\frac{13}{25} = \frac{}{100}$

5. 0.5% of n = 0. _____ n

6. 0.15 = _____ %

7. _____ % = $\frac{4}{5}$ = 0.8

10. $\frac{n}{100} =$ _____ % = 0.52

12. $\frac{2}{5} = \frac{}{45}$

13. 90% of 100 = _____

15. $\frac{1}{5} =$ _____ %

16. range of 8, 6, 19, 12, 31, 30

18. 1% = 0. _____

19. 3.5 : 5 = _____ : 100

20. 0.87 = _____ %

21. $\frac{3}{4}$ = 0.75 = _____ %

22. median of 40, 45, 67, 9, 48

23. 1% of 2000 = _____

Name _____ Date _____

Geometric Word Search

Use at the beginning of the school year.

There are 25 geometry words in the grid below. The words can be
found going up, down, forward, or backward. Circle as many as
you can find. Good luck!

S	C	O	N	E	Y	—	A	X	I	S
O	T	R	O	D	I	M	A	R	Y	P
L	E	L	L	A	R	A	P	J	N	R
I	B	Y	E	C	U	B	E	P	I	E
D	I	A	G	O	N	A	L	L	I	L
T	P	R	I	S	M	L	G	A	D	G
C	O	C	T	A	G	O	N	N	A	N
E	L	A	C	S	A	Z	A	E	R	A
S	L	E	L	C	R	I	C	D	O	K
I	R	T	E	T	N	E	M	G	E	S
B	A	R	C	X	E	T	R	E	V	U

Middle School Math, Course 3
Special Activities Book

Line Segment Puzzles

Use at the beginning of the school year.

Use toothpicks or pencils that are all the same size to make the figure shown. Move or eliminate segments to form the new figure.

1. Move 3 segments to form 3 congruent squares.

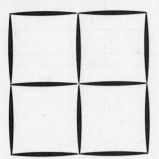

2. Move 4 segments to form 3 congruent squares.

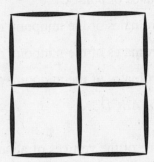

3. Move 4 segments to form 2 squares. The squares do not have to be the same size.

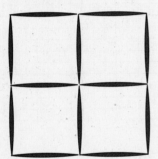

4. Eliminate 8 segments to form 2 squares. Again, the squares do not have to be the same size.

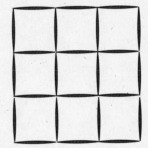

5. Move 2 segments to form 7 squares.

6. Move 3 segments to form 5 triangles.

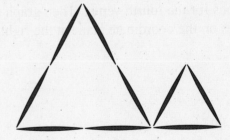

Coordinate Plane Puzzlers

Use at the beginning of the school year.

Solve.

The sides of *ABCD* are parallel to the axes of
a coordinate plane.

1. Name the coordinates of point *C*.

2. What are the coordinates of the midpoint of $\overline{AB}$?

3. What are the coordinates of the midpoint of $\overline{CD}$?

4. What are the coordinates of the midpoint of $\overline{BC}$?

5. What is the area of *ABCD*?

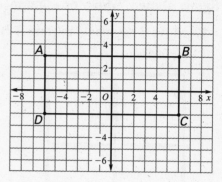

6. The points for three of the vertices of a parallelogram
have these coordinates: (4, 1), (0, 5), and (0, 0). Give
the coordinates of three possible positions for the
fourth vertex. Then graph the vertices on the coordinate
plane at the right.

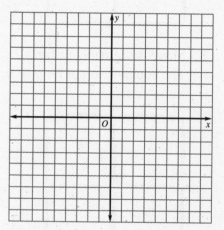

7. The points for three of the vertices of another
parallelogram have these coordinates: (7, 4), (5, 0),
and (1, 2). Give the coordinates of three possible
positions for the fourth vertex. Then graph the
vertices on the coordinate plane at the right.

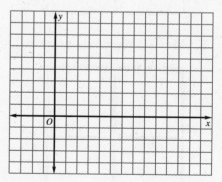

8. In which quadrant would points be located if the coordinates had
these signs?

   a. (+, +) _____   **b.** (−, −) _____

   c. (+, −) _____   **d.** (−, +) _____

CHAPTER 1

Name _____ Date _____

Coded Alphabet-Substitution Message

Use after Lesson 1.4.

Evaluate the expressions below for $x = 3$ and $y = 5$.

1. $4y - xy$ _____ Answer: _____

2. $y^2 - x$ _____ Answer: _____

3. $2x - y$ _____ Answer: _____

4. $3y - x$ _____ Answer: _____

5. $6y - (x + y) - 1$ _____ Answer: _____

6. $(3y) \div (5x)$ _____ Answer: _____

7. $y^2 - (2x - 1)$ _____ Answer: _____

8. $x^2 - (y - 1)$ _____ Answer: _____

9. $(y - 1)^2$ _____ Answer: _____

10. $10x - 3y$ _____ Answer: _____

11. $x + 4y$ _____ Answer: _____

12. $x + (y - x)$ _____ Answer: _____

13. $2x^2$ _____ Answer: _____

14. $y^2 - x^2 + 3$ _____ Answer: _____

Use your answers to Exercises 1–14 and the code 1 = a, 2 = b, 3 = c, and so on. Write the corresponding letter of the alphabet next to each answer. The letters, written in order from 1–14, spell the words that complete the statement.

When you follow the correct order of operations, first compute inside the parentheses, then _____ _____ before multiplying in order from left to right.

Write expressions similar to those in Exercises 1–14. Then write the answers. Make sure the answers match the appropriate letter of the alphabet. The letters should spell out the word that completes the following statement.

10^3 has _____ zeros.

15. _____ Answer: _____

16. _____ Answer: _____

17. _____ Answer: _____

18. _____ Answer: _____

19 _____ Answer: _____

Trade papers with a friend to check your work.

Name _____ Date _____

Hidden Words Puzzle
Use after Lesson 1.7.

In the grid below write the word that completes each statement.

Clues

1. Each bar in a _____ indicates the frequency of an interval.

2. A _____ is a symbol, usually a letter, that represents one or more numbers.

3. _____ are information, facts, or numbers that describe something.

4. How often a specific item occurs within an interval of time is called the _____.

5. Two _____ separated by an equals sign is called an equation.

6. In the equation $8 + x = 10$, $x = 2$ is the _____ of the equation.

7. 5 is the _____ in the expression 2^5.

8. _____ is a measure expressed in square units.

9. Each bar in a _____ indicates the count of an event or inequality.

10. To _____ $6(3 + 2)$, first add 3 and 2, then multiply the sum by 6.

11. In an _____ , the quantities on each side of the equals sign have the same value.

12. _____ is the measure of the distance around a figure.

13. To _____ $x + 6 = 24$, think *what number plus 6 equals 24?*

14. The most common grouping symbols are _____ .

15. In the expression 2^5, the number 2 is the _____.

Read the two words within the gray column to complete the following sentence.

When you solve an equation, you must follow the correct _____ of _____.

Middle School Math, Course 3
Special Activities Book

CHAPTER 2

Name _____ Date _____

Number Line Message

Use after Lesson 2.5.

Write the value of each expression.

1. $-15 + 5$ _____ A

2. $-5 + 9$ _____ A

3. $3 \times (-3)$ _____ B

4. $(-7 + 3) + 4$ _____ E

5. $-16 \div (-2)$ _____ E

6. $-3 - 2$ _____ L

7. $-10 \div (-2)$ _____ L

8. $(-7 - 3) + 4$ _____ O

9. $-12 + 5$ _____ S

10. $8 + (-10)$ _____ T

11. $5 + (-9)$ _____ U

12. $12 + (-5)$ _____ U

13. $-8 - (-10)$ _____ V

Use your answers to Exercises 1–13 to fill in the number line below. Write the letter related to each value above its place on the number line. Your message should make the following sentence true.

Both 6 and -6 have the same _____.

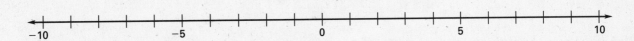

Write expressions similar to those in Exercises 1–13. The answers should spell out "integer". Write your own statement that can be completed by the word "integer".

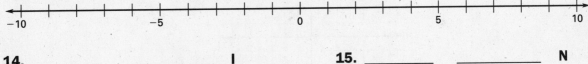

14. _____ _____ I

15. _____ _____ N

16. _____ _____ T

17. _____ _____ E

18. _____ _____ G

19. _____ _____ E

20. _____ _____ R

Name _____ Date _____

Coordinate Message

Use after Lesson 2.8.

For each set below, use the coordinates of the previous point as values of *x* and *y* to find the next point. Connect the points for each set in the order in which you plot them on the coordinate plane.

Set 1	Set 2	Set 3	Set 4
A. Start at $(-5, -2)$	**A.** Start at $(-2, -2)$	**A.** Start at $(2, -2)$	**A.** Start at $(4, 2)$
B. $(x, y + 4)$	**B.** $(x + 1, y + 4)$	**B.** $(x, y + 4)$	**B.** $(x, y - 4)$
C. $(x + 1, y - 2)$	**C.** $(x + 1, y - 2)$	**C.** $(x - 1, y)$	**C.** $(x, y + 2)$
D. $(x + 1, y + 2)$	**D.** $(x - 2, y)$	**D.** $(x + 2, y)$	**D.** $(x + 2, y)$
E. $(x, y - 4)$	**E.** $(x + 2, y)$		**E.** $(x, y + 2)$
	F. $(x + 1, y - 2)$		**F.** $(x, y - 4)$

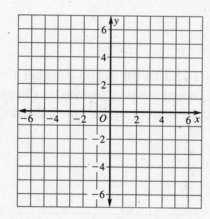

Plot your own coordinate message for a friend to decode.

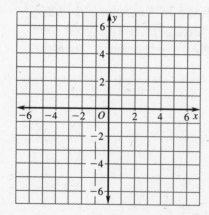

CHAPTER 3

Name _____ Date _____

Hidden Message

Use after Lesson 3.4.

Solve each equation.

1. $a + 25 = 38$ _____

2. $e + (-7) = -10$ _____

3. $5e = 0$ _____

4. $\dfrac{e}{10} = 1$ _____

5. $\dfrac{i}{10} = (-1)$ _____

6. $5i = 100$ _____

7. $-2n = 11$ _____

8. $-4n = -100$ _____

9. $o \div 4 = 5.5$ _____

10. $o + 10o = 11$ _____

11. $4p = 22$ _____

12. $4.8 \div r = -2$ _____

13. $-r + 12.6 = 0$ _____

14. $-2s = 3.6$ _____

15. $1.5s = 45$ _____

16. $t - (-6) = 21.5$ _____

17. $-10v = 42$ _____

Write each value from Exercises 1–17 in order, from least to greatest. In that order, write the variable in the grid below. This will give you a term that makes the following sentence true.

To undo operations, use _____   _____ .

Value																	
Variable																	

Name _____ Date _____

Hidden Words Puzzle

Use after Lesson 3.7.

In the grid below write the word that completes each statement.

Figure 1

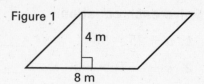

Clues

1. Addition and subtraction are ____ operations.

2. $2 < 3$ is an ____.

3. $x = 6$ is the ____ of $x + 6 = 12$.

4. In Figure 1 above, 4 m is the ____.

5. In $t + 17 = 42$, the ____ of t is 25.

6. In Figure 1 above, 8 m is the ____.

7. To ____ the expression $6x + 4x + 3$, first combine like terms.

8. The opposite of positive 6 is ____ 6.

9. In $A = \ell w$, the ℓ represents the ____ of a rectangle.

10. To undo division, ____.

11. Is (-1) the opposite of 1? ____

12. The number 6 ____ half of 12.

13. To undo addition, ____.

14. To undo subtraction, ____.

15. To evaluate $6x$, when $x = 4$, first ____ 4 for x, then multiply.

16. Three times ten equals ____.

17. When you ____ an equation, you find the value of the variable.

18. ____ is one less than ninety-one.

19. If $6x = 36$, the value of x is ____.

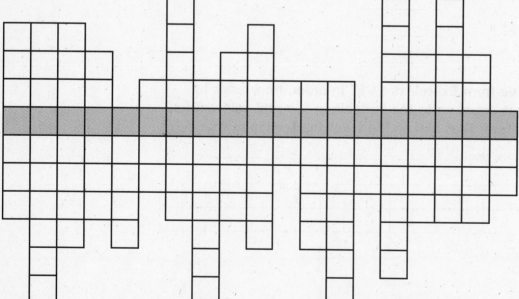

Read the phrase within the gray row to complete the following sentence.

When the values of the variables of two equations are always the same, then they are _____ .

Name _____ Date _____

Coded Message
Use after Lesson 4.4.

Write your answers in the answer column.

		Answer
1. What is the least prime number?		_____ = T
2. What is the greatest common factor of 15 and 30?		_____ = N
3. What is the simplest mixed-number form of $\frac{5}{2}$?		_____ = C
4. What is the simplest mixed-number form of $\frac{107}{4}$?		_____ = L
5. What is the simplest form of $\frac{20}{25}$?		_____ = E
6. What is the number whose prime factorization is $2^3 \times 5$?		_____ = P
7. What is the greatest one-digit prime number?		_____ = M
8. What is the number that has the prime factorization $2 \times 3 \times 5$?		_____ = T
9. What is the simplest mixed-number form of $\frac{56}{5}$?		_____ = O
10. What is a fraction equivalent to $\frac{1}{2}$?		_____ = L
11. What is the greatest two-digit prime number?		_____ = E
12. What is the least two-digit prime number?		_____ = M
13. What is the square of the least sum of two primes?		_____ = U
14. What is the greatest common factor of 6 and 7?		_____ = A
15. What is the least common multiple of 4 and 9?		_____ = I
16. What is the greatest common factor of 40 and 60?		_____ = M
17. What is the simplest mixed-number form of $\frac{25}{20}$?		_____ = S
18. What is the number whose prime factorization is $2^2 \times 19$?		_____ = L
19. What is the monomial in this list: $3, 3x + 2, 6x - 5$?		_____ = O

Use your answers to Exercises 1–19 to complete the statement below. First, order your answers from least to greatest. Then place the matching letter next to its value to spell out the missing words.

Statement:

The _____ _____ _____ of two
numbers is the least number that is a common multiple of both
of them.

Name _____ Date _____

Hidden Term

Use after Lesson 4.8.

Write in the grid below the word that completes each statement.

1. The abbreviation for *greatest common factor* is _____ .

2. A _____ number has exactly two factors.

3. _____ is the least two-digit prime number.

4. When the greatest common factor of two numbers is 1, then the two numbers are said to be _____ prime.

5. All _____ of 6 have 6 as a factor.

6. A mathematical phrase that uses numerals and operation symbols is called a _____ expression.

7. The _____ common denominator of two fractions is the least common multiple of the two denominators.

8. The prime factorization of _____ is $2^3 \times 5$.

9. When you multiply two or more _____, you get a product.

10. A _____ is a number, a variable, or a product of a number and one or more variables.

11. When the numerator and denominator of a fraction have only 1 as their greatest common factor, the fraction is in _____ form.

12. _____ numbers have more than two factors.

13. The number _____ is neither prime nor composite.

14. When 9400 is written 9.4×10^3, the number is written in _____ notation.

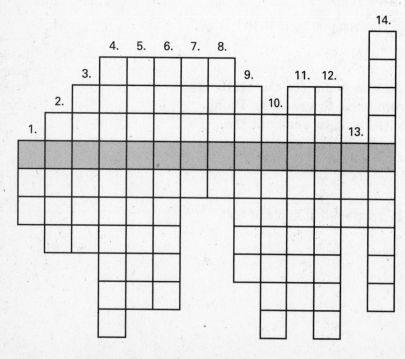

Complete the statement below using the phrase within the gray row.

Eleven is the _____

_____ factor of 121

and 132.

CHAPTER 5

Matching Expressions

Use after Lesson 5.4.

Write the letter of the equivalent expression on the rule next to each exercise. Some answers will be used more than once.

1. $-4 + 1\frac{1}{6}$ _____

2. $\frac{1}{14} + \frac{1}{7}$ _____

3. $-2(2x)$ _____

4. $\frac{1}{2} \times \frac{3}{7}$ _____

5. $-1\frac{8}{9} \div \frac{2}{3}$ _____

6. $\frac{8}{21} - \frac{1}{6}$ _____

7. $\frac{1}{2}(-8)$ _____

8. $2\left(\frac{x}{3}\right)$ _____

9. $17 \cdot \frac{1}{2}$ _____

10. $-2\left(1\frac{5}{6}\right)$ _____

11. $2\left(1\frac{5}{6}\right)$ _____

12. $3\left(\frac{x}{12}\right)$ _____

13. $\frac{1}{2}(8)$ _____

14. $7\frac{1}{3} - 3\frac{2}{3}$ _____

15. $2\frac{1}{4}\left(\frac{1}{4} \cdot 4\right)$ _____

16. $\frac{1}{3} \div \frac{1}{11}$ _____

17. $\frac{1}{3}$ of $\frac{3}{4}$ _____

18. $\frac{3}{8} \cdot \frac{4}{7}$ _____

19. $\frac{1}{3}$ of $\frac{-3}{4}$ _____

20. $\left(-4\frac{1}{2}\right) + 6\frac{3}{4}$ _____

21. $\frac{3}{4}(8x)$ _____

22. $\left(\frac{-1}{3}\right)\left(\frac{-3}{4}\right)$ _____

23. $\frac{1}{4}$ of 18 _____

24. $4 - 1\frac{1}{6}$ _____

A. $4\frac{1}{2}$	
C. $\frac{1}{4}$	
D. $-2\frac{5}{6}$	
E. $3\frac{2}{3}$	
G. $\frac{2x}{3}$	
H. 4	
I. $\frac{3}{14}$	
L. $2\frac{5}{6}$	
N. -4	
O. $6x$	
P. $\frac{-1}{4}$	
R. $2\frac{1}{4}$	
S. $-3\frac{2}{3}$	
T. $\frac{x}{4}$	
U. $8\frac{1}{2}$	
V. $-4x$	

Write the letter of the answer above each exercise number below to find the math message.

D __ __ __ __ __ __ __   ? __ __ __   __ __ __
  1 2 3 4 5 6 7 8   9 10 11   12 13 14

__ __ __ __ __ __ __ __ __ __ !
15 16 17 18 19 20 21 22 23 24

Box Scores

Use after Lesson 5.8.

Use the numbers in the box to complete each exercise.
For Exercises 1–4 use each number once.

3.16	3	2.6	12	
	$\frac{1}{3}$	−1.845	−6$\frac{1}{2}$	−6.49

1. Write an addition expression whose value is greater than 1 but less than 2.   _____

2. Write a multiplication expression whose value is between 7 and 8.   _____

3. Write a division expression whose value is greater than 20.   _____

4. Write a subtraction expression whose value is as close as possible to 0.   _____

5. Order the numbers in the box from least to greatest.   _____

6. Find the median of the numbers in the box. Round to the nearest hundredth.   _____

7. Find the mean of the numbers in the box. Round to the nearest hundredth.   _____

8. Find the range of the numbers in the box.   _____

9. Which number in the box can be written as a repeating decimal?   _____

In the empty box, write eight numbers that answer Exercises 10–13. Give your work to a friend to solve.

10. Write an addition expression whose value is greater than 1.   _____

11. Write a multiplication expression whose value is between 7 and 8.   _____

12. Write a division expression whose value is greater than 20.   _____

13. Write a subtraction expression whose value is as close as possible to 0.   _____

CHAPTER 6

Name _____ Date _____

Matching Code

Use after Lesson 6.3.

Solve each equation, and then write the letter of the solution.
Some answers will be used more than once.

Exercise

1. $4(x + 2) = 20$

2. $4(x - 2) = 20$

3. $4(2 - x) = 20$

4. $\frac{3}{4}x = -\frac{1}{4}x + 4$

5. $\frac{3}{4}x = \frac{1}{4}x - 3$

6. $-\frac{3}{4}x = -\frac{1}{4}x - 3$

7. $1.5x - 2 = 13$

8. $1.5x + 3 = 15$

9. $1.5x - 4 = -13$

10. $1.5(x - 4) = 7.5$

11. $\frac{1}{8}x - 5 = \left(-\frac{3}{8}x\right)$

12. $-7x = -7$

13. $\frac{1}{10}(-7x) = -7$

14. $16x = 4$

15. $15x = -45$

16. $60x = -12x + 36$

Answer

B. $x = 4$

C. $x = 3$

E. $x = 10$

I. $x = -6$

K. $x = 9$

L. $x = 8$

M. $x = -3$

N. $x = 6$

O. $x = 7$

R. $x = \frac{1}{4}$

S. $x = 0.5$

T. $x = 1$

Use your answers to Exercises 1–16 to complete the statement
below. Write the letter of each answer to complete the math term
that makes the statement true.

$$\frac{\text{c}}{1 \ \ 2 \ \ 3 \ \ 4 \ \ 5 \ \ 6 \ \ 7} \qquad \frac{}{8 \ \ 9 \ \ 10 \ \ 11} \qquad \frac{}{12 \ \ 13 \ \ 14 \ \ 15 \ \ 16}$$

Statement:

The first step in simplifying an expression or equation

is to _____ _____ _____.

Name _____ Date _____

Figure a Message

Use after Lesson 6.6.

Use these diagrams for Exercises 1–10. Use 3.14 for π.

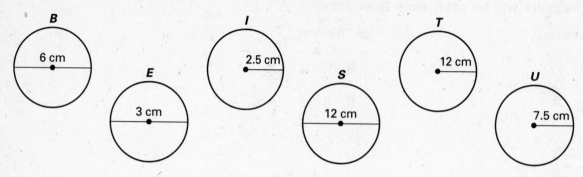

Answer

1. Which figure has $r = 6$? _____

2. For which figure does $d = 15$? _____

3. Which figure has $r = 3$? _____

4. Which figure's circumference is greater than 36 and less than 39? _____

5. For which figure is $3d > 70$? _____

6. For which figure is C greater than 15 and less than 18? _____

7. For which figure is $C + 3 \geq 75$? _____

8. For which figure is $C \approx 47$? _____

9. For which figure does $\pi\left(\dfrac{d}{8}\right) = 3\pi$? _____

10. For which figure is $d < \pi$? _____

Use your answers to Exercises 1–10 to complete the statement below. Write the letter of each answer to complete the math term that makes the statement true.

$\dfrac{\text{s}}{\overline{1 \quad 2 \quad 3 \quad 4 \quad 5 \quad 6 \quad 7 \quad 8 \quad 9 \quad 10}}$

Statement:

To find the value of an expression, _____ a value for each variable.

Draw some different-sized circles. Label the radius or diameter of each circle. Then write your own circle clues for the math term that makes the following statement true.

Statement: To undo multiplication, _____.

Name _____ Date _____

Coded Message

Use after Lesson 7.4.

Solve each proportion. Write your answer on the rule next to each exercise.

Exercise	Answer
1. $\dfrac{1 \text{ inch}}{10 \text{ feet}} = \dfrac{5 \text{ inches}}{a \text{ feet}}$	$a = $ _____
2. $\dfrac{1 \text{ ounce}}{2 \text{ quarts}} = \dfrac{c \text{ ounces}}{6 \text{ quarts}}$	$c = $ _____
3. $1 \text{ feet} : 10 \text{ mile} = d \text{ feet} : 5 \text{ miles}$	$d = $ _____
4. $\dfrac{130 \text{ miles}}{2 \text{ hours}} = \dfrac{e \text{ miles}}{1 \text{ hour}}$	$e = $ _____
5. 10 hours is to 1 trip as ℓ hours is to 7 trips	$\ell = $ _____
6. $\dfrac{4 \text{ quarts}}{1 \text{ gallon}} = \dfrac{o \text{ quarts}}{\frac{3}{4} \text{ gallon}}$	$o = $ _____
7. $\dfrac{p \text{ miles}}{3 \text{ gallons}} = \dfrac{23\frac{1}{3} \text{ miles}}{1 \text{ gallon}}$	$p = $ _____
8. $\dfrac{30 \text{ dollars}}{100 \text{ min}} = \dfrac{6 \text{ dollars}}{q \text{ min}}$	$q = $ _____
9. $\dfrac{15 \text{ min}}{2 \text{ miles}} = \dfrac{3\frac{3}{4} \text{ min}}{r \text{ miles}}$	$r = $ _____
10. $\dfrac{6 \text{ drops}}{s \text{ gallons}} = \dfrac{18 \text{ drops}}{9 \text{ gallons}}$	$s = $ _____
11. $\dfrac{t \text{ dollars}}{1 \text{ day}} = \dfrac{140 \text{ dollars}}{7 \text{ days}}$	$t = $ _____
12. $\dfrac{20 \text{ dollars}}{1 \text{ pound}} = \dfrac{u \text{ dollars}}{7 \text{ pounds}}$	$u = $ _____

Use your answers to Exercises 1–12 to complete the statement below. To find a true statement about proportions, write each variable above its value in the boxes below.

The | | | | | |
3 oz $\frac{1}{2}$ mi   3 qt   3 gal   3 gal

| | | | | | | | |
70 mi $\frac{1}{2}$ mi   3 qt $\frac{1}{2}$ ft $140   3 oz $20   3 gal

| | | | | | | | |
50 ft $\frac{1}{2}$ mi   65 mi   65 mi   20 min $140   50 ft   70 h

Middle School Math, Course 3 23
Special Activities Book

Name _____ Date _____

Word Maze

Use after Lesson 7.8.

Read each statement. Write the word that makes the statement true in the maze below.

1. The _____ of inches to feet on a yardstick is 1 : 12.

2. An _____ is a possible result of an experiment.

3. Two _____ ratios form a proportion.

4. Six is to twelve as _____ is to six.

5. A ratio of quantities with different units is called a _____.

6. The top number in a fraction or ratio is the _____.

7. *Across:* An equation showing two equal ratios is a _____.

7. *Down:* A ratio with a denominator of 100 is a _____.

8. When you calculate the probability of an event without doing any experiments, this is called _____ probability.

9. $\dfrac{3 \text{ dollars}}{4 \text{ liters}} = \dfrac{6 \text{ dollars}}{8}$

10. A _____ is the relationship between the dimensions of a model and the object.

11. Three : four = six : _____.

12. A _____ is usually the percent taken off the regular price of an item.

13. 1 minute : 60 seconds = $\frac{1}{60}$ minute : 1 _____.

14. *Across:* When a tax is applied to a purchase, the cost of the item _____.

14. *Down:* $\dfrac{6 \text{ dollars}}{3 \text{ inches}} = \dfrac{2 \text{ dollars}}{1 \_\_\_\_}$.

15. $\dfrac{10 \text{ fingers}}{2 \text{ hands}} = \dfrac{5 \text{ fingers}}{1 \_\_\_\_}$

16. When items are on sale, "6% off" means the cost of the items _____.

17. An _____ is a collection of outcomes.

18. _____ : fifty = forty : one hundred

Middle School Math, Course 3
Special Activities Book

Name _____ Date _____

Missing Angles

Use after Lesson 8.4.

Use the rules for supplementary angles and vertical angles to find each angle measure. Note that there are no parallel lines in the figure.

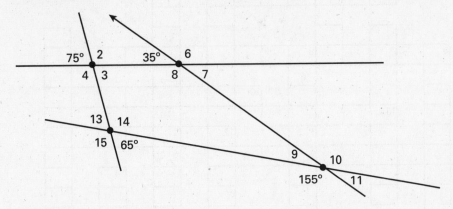

1. $m\angle 2$ _____° = o   2. $m\angle 3$ _____° = c

3. $m\angle 14$ _____° = e   4. $m\angle 13$ _____° = s

5. $m\angle 6$ _____° = 1   6. $m\angle 7$ _____° = m

7. $m\angle 10$ _____° = t   8. $m\angle 9$ _____° = p

9. $m\angle 3 + m\angle 8 + m\angle 9 + m\angle 14 =$ _____° = n

Use your answers to Exercises 1–8 to complete the statement below. Locate each angle measure below. Write the related letter to spell out the missing term.

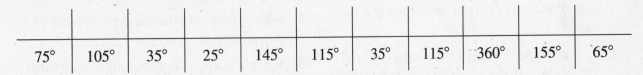

75°	105°	35°	25°	145°	115°	35°	115°	360°	155°	65°

Statement: In a right triangle, the two acute angles are _____.

Use a ruler and a protractor to make your own missing angles puzzle. The answers should spell the term that completes the statement below. Trade with a friend and solve.

Statement: A polygon whose angles have a sum of 180° is a _____.

10. $m\angle$ ___ _____° = i   11. $m\angle$ ___ _____° = e

12. $m\angle$ ___ _____° = r   13. $m\angle$ ___ _____° = l

14. $m\angle$ ___ _____° = a   15. $m\angle$ ___ _____° = n

16. $m\angle$ ___ _____° = g   17. $m\angle$ ___ _____° = t

Name _____ Date _____

Crossword Puzzle

Use after Lesson 8.8.

Use the clues to complete the puzzle.

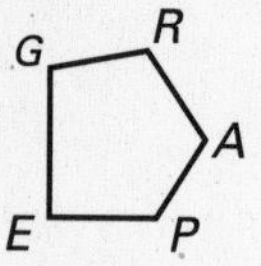

G R
A
E P

Figure A

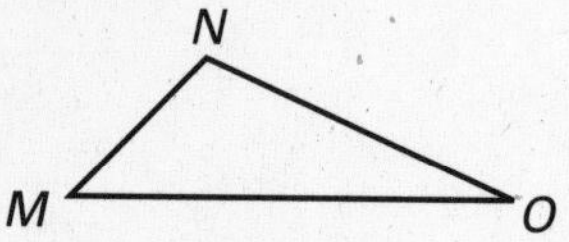

N

M O

Figure B

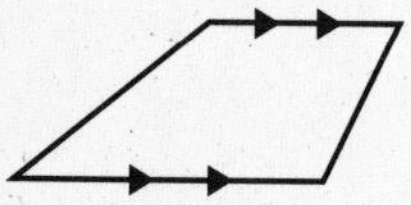

Figure C

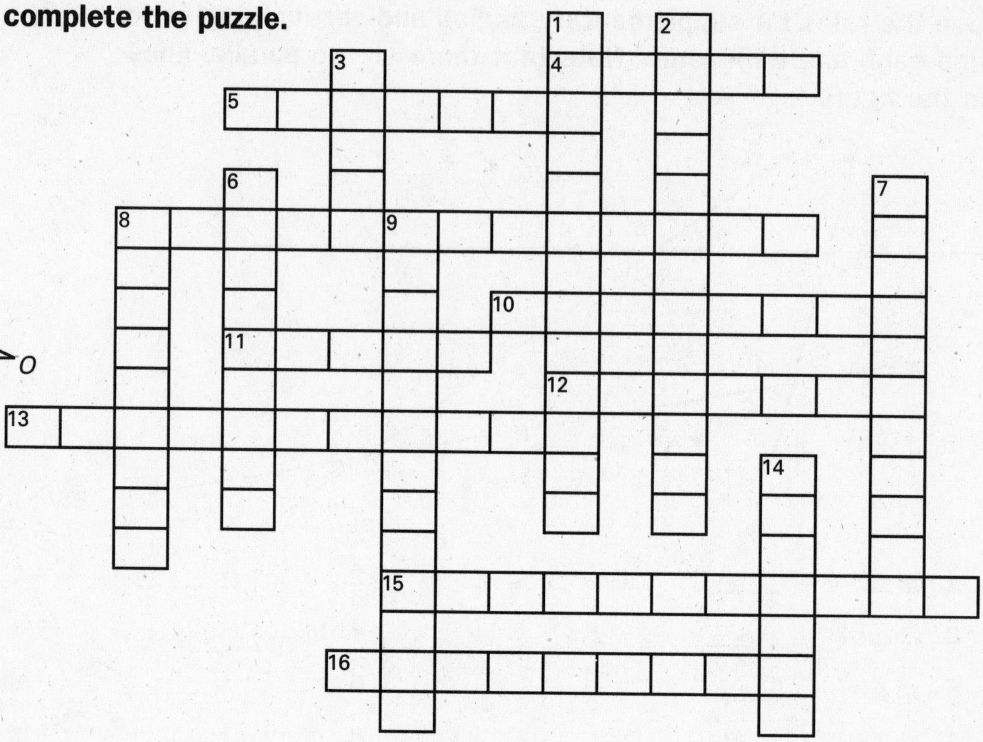

Clues

Across

4. When two expressions have the same value, they are _____.

5. When two plane figures have congruent angles and proportional sides they are also called _____ figures.

8. Two congruent triangles are labeled △ABC and △QRS. If ∠A ≅ ∠Q and ∠B ≅ ∠R, then ∠C is _____ to ∠S.

10. A transformation that enlarges or reduces a figure proportionally

11. Write the name of Figure A such that the letters also name a juicy fruit.

12. When two expressions *do not* have the same value, they are _____.

13. When each of the three sides of a triangle measure 3 cm, the triangle is _____.

15. The name for Figure B is _____.

16. What type of quadrilateral is Figure C?

Down

1. Two lines that intersect at a right angle are _____.

2. A _____ is a four-sided plane figure.

3. When you hold your hand up in front of a mirror, you see a mirror _____.

6. When a polygon does *not* have congruent sides it is called an _____ polygon.

7. A transformation that moves every point of a figure the same distance and direction

8. Another way to describe two angles that each measure 76° is to say they are _____.

9. Two angles whose measures have a sum of 180° are _____.

14. The numbers that are added to get a sum are called.

Name _____ Date _____

Matching Code

Use after Lesson 9.4.

**Solve each equation. Write the matching letter on the blank.
Some letters will be used more than once.**

1. $x^2 - 14 = 2$ _____
2. $x^2 + 36 = 61$ _____
3. $-24 + x^2 = 1$ _____
4. $x^2 = 169$ _____
5. $48 + x^2 = 52$ _____
6. $x^2 + 16 = 32$ _____
7. $x^2 + 25 = 89$ _____
8. $-32 + x^2 = 68$ _____
9. $72 + x^2 = 241$ _____
10. $x^2 - 17 = 64$ _____
11. $x^2 + 27 = 127$ _____
12. $-17 + x^2 = 19$ _____
13. $2x^2 - 18 = 0$ _____
14. $2x^2 - 42 = 200$ _____
15. $x^2 + 25 = 74$ _____
16. $-17 + x^2 = 8$ _____

A. ± 13
B. ± 11
E. ± 7
I. ± 4
L. ± 9
M. ± 3
N. ± 10
O. ± 8
R. ± 5
T. ± 2
U. ± 6

**Use your answers to Exercises 1–16 to complete the statement
below. Write the letter of each answer to find the terms that
makes the statement true.**

____ ____ ____ ____ ____ ____ ____ ____ ____ ____
1.   2.   3.   4.   5.   6.   7.   8.   9.   10.

____ ____ ____ ____ ____ ____
11.   12.   13.   14.   15.   16.

Statement: If a whole number is not a perfect square, then its square root
is an _____ _____.

Name _____ Date _____

Word Maze
Use after Lesson 9.6.

Use the clues to find the word or phrase that starts in the box
with the same number as the clue. All words or phrases start and
end in gray boxes. Answers with more than one word do not have
spaces between the words.

1. The theorem that relates the sides of right triangles

2. $\sqrt{26}$ is an irrational ____.

3. Rational and irrational numbers are all ____ numbers.

4. A ____ of a right triangle has one end point at the right angle.

5. $\sqrt{25}$ is ____ than $\sqrt{16}$.

6. eight squared

7. The ratios in right triangles that compare the side opposite to an angle to the hypotenuse

8. *Across:* The ratios in a right triangle that compare the side adjacent to an angle to the hypotenuse

8. *Down:* When you reverse the *if* and *then* parts of a statement, you create the ____ of the statement.

9. When two measurements are ____, they have the same value.

10. Order $\sqrt{8}$, 4, and $\sqrt{9}$. $\sqrt{8}$ is ____.

11. the ratio of the side opposite to the side adjacent to an angle of a right triangle

12. A ____ is a statement of a mathematical generalization.

13. $a^2 + b^2 = c^2$ is equivalent to c^2 ____ $a^2 = b^2$.

14. Radical signs indicate ____.

15. If $x > \pm \sqrt{25}$, then x is ____ greater than 5 or less than −5.

16. the longest side of a right triangle

Name _____ Date _____

Matching Code

Use after Lesson 10.3.

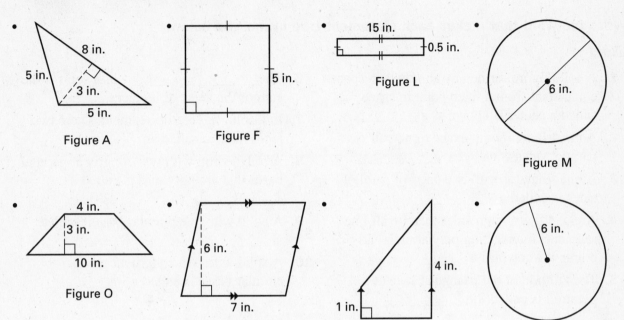

Figure A

Figure F

Figure L

Figure M

Figure O

Figure R

Figure S

Figure U

Write the letter of each figure next to its area. Use 3.14 for π.

____ **1.** 25 square inches

____ **2.** 21 square inches

____ **3.** 42 square inches

____ **4.** 28.26 square inches

____ **5.** 113.04 square inches

____ **6.** 7.5 square inches

____ **7.** 12 square inches

____ **8.** 6.25 square inches

Use your answers to Exercises 1–8. Read the figure letters in order from top to bottom. They will spell out the term that makes the following statement true.

Statement: To find the area of many plane figures, you can use

_____.

9. Make a puzzle similar to the one above. Your term should make the following statement true. The two bases of a _____ are congruent polygons.

Name _____ Date _____

Hidden Word Puzzle

Use after Lesson 10.7.

Write the word that makes each statement true in the grid below.

Clues

1. A solid figure formed by all points in space equidistant from a fixed point in space called a center is known as a _____.

2. A quadrilateral with exactly one pair of parallel sides is called a _____.

3. A quadrilateral with two pairs of parallel sides is called a _____.

4. A plane figure with sides that are all line segments intersecting only at their end-points is known as a _____.

5. The altitude of the triangular face of a pyramid is called the _____ _____.

6. The _____ _____ of a solid is the sum of the areas of its faces.

7. In a solid figure, the segment where two faces meet is called an _____.

8. A polyhedron with two congruent parallel bases that are polygons is called a _____.

9. A solid with one circular base is called a _____.

10. A solid with two congruent parallel circular bases is called a _____.

Check:

Read the phrase within the gray column to complete the following statement.

Statement: A three-dimensional figure with faces that are all polygons is a _____.

11. Make a puzzle similar to the one above. Make the letters in the gray squares spell the word that makes the following statement true.

    Statement: The _____ of a cylinder are not polygons.

12.
13.
14.
15.
16.

Name _____ Date _____

Function Flag

Use after Lesson 11.4.

For each exercise, write an equation that relates the two variables.

1.

x	2	4	6	8
y	8	6	4	2

_____

2.

x	0	2	4	6
y	6	4	2	0

_____

3.

x	4	6	8	10
y	10	8	6	4

_____

4.

x	0	2	4	6
y	2	4	6	8

_____

5.

x	2	4	6	8
y	0	2	4	6

_____

6.

x	6	8	9	10
y	0	2	3	4

_____

7.

x	0	2	3	4
y	6	8	9	10

_____

8. Use the tables from Exercises 1–7. For each table, graph each ordered pair. Connect the points.

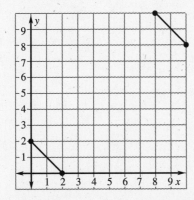

9. On a separate sheet of graph paper, draw another first quadrant coordinate plane. Draw 7 lines to make another pattern of intersecting diagonal lines. Make a table of x and y values for the several points on each line. Using two variables, write an equation that describes each line.

Name _____ Date _____

Hidden Message

Use after Lesson 11.8.

Write in the grid below the word that completes each statement.

Clues:

1. A _____ equation in two variables is an equation in which the variables appear in separate terms and each variable occurs only to the first power.

2. In a function, for each _____, there is exactly one output.

3. A _____ plot is the graph of a collection of ordered pairs.

4. All functions are _____, but not all _____ are functions.

5. An _____ _____ describes a point on a coordinate grid.

6. The line described by $x = 3$ shows that this equation does *not* represent a _____ because for each value of x, there is more than one value of y.

7. The _____ of a nonvertical line is noted by its vertical change.

8. The _____ of a line is the ratio rise : run.

9. In (x, y), the x is the input, and y is the _____.

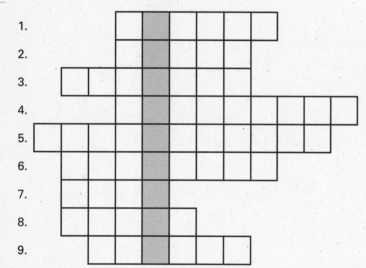

10. Read the phrase within the gray column to complete the following statement.

Statement:

The y-_____ of the line described by $y = 2x + 4$ is 4.

11. Make your own hidden-message puzzle. The term in the gray column should make the following statement true.

Statement:

The _____ of a function is the set of all possible output values.

Name _____ Date _____

Graphic Message

Use after Lesson 12.3.

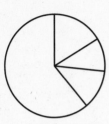

Graph I

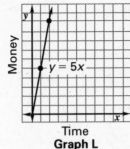

Graph L

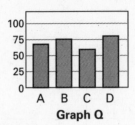

Graph Q

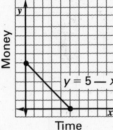

Graph R

Graph T

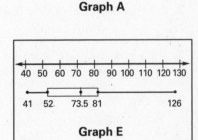

Graph U

Match each graph or plot with its data set.

1. Mean test scores for four students

2. Votes for president: Jane: 47, John: 72, Juan: 80, Jerry: 51

3. Cars entering an intersection each hour for 10 hours:

    50, 36, 48, 43, 51, 54, 49, 34, 31, 50

4. Number of students scoring in each range of test scores in a class of 37

5. Money left after x hours of paying to play video games

6. Money spent by the soccer team: uniforms: $1500, balls: $250, referees: $300, protective gear: $400

7. Money earned after x hours of work if paid by the hour

8. Basketball game scores for 10 games:

    50, 75, 41, 52, 80, 92, 67, 72, 126, 81

9. Write the matching letters for Exercises 1–8 in order, to complete the statement below.

The lower _____ is the median of the lower half of an ordered set of data.

```
3 | 1 4 6
4 | 3 8 9
5 | 0 0 1 4
```
Graph A

```
  40  50  60  70  80  90  100 110 120 130
  41  52   73.5 81                  126
```
Graph E

Name _____ Date _____

Crossword Puzzle

Use after Lesson 12.8.

Write in the puzzle below the word that completes each statement.

Clues

Across

2. The ratio of favorable outcomes to unfavorable outcomes gives the _____ of an event.

4. In a box-and-whisker plot, the ____ encloses the middle half of the data.

5. If the outcome of one event influences the outcome of another, the two events are ____.

7. An arrangement in which order *is* important is called a _____.

10. If the outcome of one event does not influence the outcome of another, the two events are ____.

11. The ____-___-____ data organizing method allows you to see how data are distributed.

12. The probability of an event that is certain is equal to _____.

Down

1. A _____ is a group of choices whose order is *not* important.

3. Two events are ____ if one or the other *must* occur.

6. The upper ____ is the median of the upper half of the data set.

9. When you order a data set, the ____ data value is the end of the left-most whisker of a box-and-whisker plot.

Matching Polynomials

Use after Lesson 13.3.

Match each polynomial with an equivalent polynomial. You will use some answers more than once.

1. $x(2x^2)$ _____

2. $(x^3 + 3x^2 + 4x + 3) - (x^3 + 2x + 4)$ _____

3. $\frac{1}{2}(4x^2 + 4x - 4)$ _____

4. $4x^2 - 3(x^2 + 2x + 1)$ _____

5. $x^2 - 3(x^2 + 2x - 3)$ _____

6. $2(x^2 + x - 1)$ _____

7. $-\frac{1}{3}(-6x^2 - 6x - 6)$ _____

8. $9 - 2x(x + 3)$ _____

9. $x^2(2x)^2$ _____

10. $x^2(-2x)$ _____

11. $2(x^2 + x + 1)$ _____

12. $(4x^2 - 8x - 4) + (-2x^2 + 2x + 13)$ _____

A. $2x^2 + 2x - 2$

D. $-2x^2 - 6x + 9$

F. $4x^4$

M. $2x^2 - 6x + 9$

N. $x^2 - 6x - 3$

O. $-2x^3$

R. $2x^2 + 2x + 2$

S. $2x^3$

T. $3x^2 + 2x - 1$

13. Read the letters of your answers to Exercises 1–12 in order from top to bottom. The letters should form the term that completes the following statement.

Statement:

A polynomial is in _____ _____ when it is written with the powers of the variables decreasing from left to right.

14. Make your own Matching Polynomials puzzle. Your term should make the following statement true.

Statement:

A _____ is a polynomial with two terms.

Name _____ Date _____

Word Maze

Use after Lesson 13.5.

Use the clues to complete the puzzle. The answer to each clue starts in the box with the same number as the clue. All words start and end in gray boxes. The letter in each gray box is part of the answers to two clues.

1. A _____ expression has one term.

2. A _____ equation in two variables is an equation in which the variables appear in separate terms and each variable occurs only to the first power.

3. In the formula $A = \pi r^2$, r represents the _____.

4. When you _____ an expression, you replace it with an equivalent expression that has the fewest terms possible.

5. $x^3 \cdot x^4 = x^7$ is an example of the product of powers _____.

6. When you _____ factors, you change their order.

7. *Across:* A _____ is any expression in the form a^n.

7. *Down:* The result of multiplication is the _____.

8. A binomial is a polynomial with two _____.

9. The _____ form of a polynomial is the form in which the terms are in order of decreasing degree.

10. You can use the distributive property to multiply or _____ polynomials.

11. To _____ the expression $(2x^2)(4x)$, write $2 \cdot x \cdot x \cdot 4 \cdot x$.

12. x times x equals x _____.

13. *Across:* Monomials, binomials, and trinomials are algebraic expressions called _____.

13. *Down:* Solutions to functions are written as ordered _____.

14. $(5, 4)$ is a _____ to $y = x^2 - 21$.

15. Function _____ for $y = 3x - 4$ is $f(x) = 3x - 4$.

16. The point described by $(5, 4)$ is _____ on the line described by $y = x + 1$.

36 **Middle School Math, Course 3**
Special Activities Book

Name _____ Date _____

Using Integers

Use before Thanksgiving.

Follow the instructions to complete each set of exercises.

1. Use the numbers 1–8 to list these temperatures from coldest to warmest.

12°F _____

−2°F _____

32°F _____

0°F _____

12° below 0°F _____

−9°F _____

38°F _____

1° below 0°F _____

2. Use the numbers 1–8 to list these golf scores in order from best (lowest) to worst (highest). *Think:* Par is an expected score. *Under par* is better than *over par*.

3 over par _____

3 under par _____

1 over par _____

6 under par _____

par _____

5 over par _____

5 under par _____

1 under par _____

3. Use the numbers 1–8 to list the dates from most recent to most ancient.

22 B.C. _____

4 A.D. _____

200 B.C. _____

22 A.D. _____

1855 A.D. _____

1911 A.D. _____

3 A.D. _____

1776 A.D. _____

4. Use the numbers 1–8 to list these elevations from highest to lowest.

150 ft above sea level _____

200 ft below sea level _____

1 mi above sea level _____

sea level _____

$\frac{1}{2}$ mi below sea level _____

$\frac{1}{4}$ mi above sea level _____

1800 ft above sea level _____

2000 ft below sea level _____

Multiples Logic

Use before Thanksgiving.

Circle I contains multiples of 3.

Circle II contains multiples of 5.

Circle III contains multiples of 8.

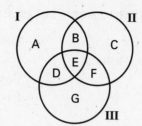

Write the letter of the region in which each number below would appear.

1. 6 _____	**2.** 25 _____	**3.** 16 _____	**4.** 30 _____
5. 20 _____	**6.** 32 _____	**7.** 45 _____	**8.** 135 _____
9. 60 _____	**10.** 180 _____	**11.** 75 _____	**12.** 80 _____
13. 48 _____	**14.** 240 _____	**15.** 72 _____	**16.** 144 _____

17. The LCM of 3 and 5 _____

18. The LCM of 5 and 8 _____

19. The LCM of 3 and 8 _____

20. The LCM of 3, 5, and 8 _____

Write a number that doesn't appear above that would belong in each of the regions.

21. A _____	**22.** B _____	**23.** C _____	**24.** D _____
25. E _____	**26.** F _____	**27.** G _____	

Summarize.

28. In which region do numbers that are multiples of 3, 5, and 8 appear?

_____

29. In which region do multiples of 3 and 5, but not of 8, appear?

_____

30. In which region do multiples of 5 and 8, but not of 3, appear?

_____

Equations with Fractions

Use before December vacation.

Use the fractions below to make each equation true.

$$\frac{5}{6} \quad \frac{1}{4} \quad \frac{1}{8} \quad \frac{1}{2} \quad \frac{2}{3}$$

1. _____ + _____ = $\frac{3}{4}$

2. _____ + _____ = $\frac{11}{12}$

3. _____ + _____ = $1\frac{1}{2}$

4. _____ + _____ = $1\frac{1}{6}$

5. _____ + _____ + _____ = $1\frac{11}{24}$

6. _____ − _____ = $\frac{17}{24}$

7. _____ − _____ = $\frac{5}{12}$

8. _____ − _____ = $\frac{1}{6}$

Try these.

9. _____ × _____ = $\frac{1}{32}$

10. _____ × _____ × _____ = $\frac{1}{12}$

Now use the fractions below to make each equation true.

$$\frac{3}{10} \quad \frac{3}{4} \quad \frac{3}{8} \quad \frac{1}{2} \quad \frac{2}{5}$$

11. _____ + _____ = $\frac{9}{10}$

12. _____ + _____ = $\frac{31}{40}$

13. _____ + _____ + _____ = $1\frac{1}{5}$

14. _____ + _____ + _____ = $1\frac{5}{8}$

15. _____ + _____ − _____ = $\frac{13}{20}$

16. _____ + _____ − _____ = $\frac{7}{8}$

Try these.

17. _____ × _____ = $\frac{3}{25}$

18. _____ × _____ × _____ = $\frac{3}{20}$

Rational Magic Squares
Use before December vacation.

In a magic square, the sums of the numbers in each row, column, and diagonal are the same.

You can write equations to express relationships in the magic square at the right. Here are two:

$$1.5 + 2.5 + 3.5 = 7.5$$

$$a + 1.5 + 2 = 7.5$$

a	b	c
1.5	2.5	3.5
2	d	e

Write four more equations related to this magic square.

1. _____   2. _____

3. _____   4. _____

5. Give the value of each letter.

   $a =$ _____ $b =$ _____ $c =$ _____ $d =$ _____ $e =$ _____

Use the magic square at the right.
Write four equations related to it.

−3	f	1
g	h	−4
k	m	3

6. _____

7. _____

8. _____

9. _____

10. Give the value of each letter.

   $f =$ _____ $g =$ _____ $h =$ _____ $k =$ _____ $m =$ _____

11. The magic sum is −15.
    Complete the square.

−7		
		−4
−2		

12. This magic sum is 6.
    Complete the square.

−2		−1
	−5	

Name _____ Date _____

Sabrina's Fabulous Prices

Use before winter break.

Sabrina's Fruit and Vegetable Market competes with three other markets
in the neighborhood. Sabrina wants her prices to be the lowest. To make
this happen, she figures out which of her competitors has the lowest unit
price for an item. Then she rounds that price to the nearest cent and
makes her unit price 2 cents less.

Find the price of each purchase in Sabrina's store.

	SABRINA'S COMPETITORS			
Item	Gabriella's Grocery	Fiona's Fruits	Manuel's Market	Sabrina's Low, Low Price
1.	$.30 each	4 for $1.00	3 for $.87	6 for _____
2.	3 lb for $2.67	5 lb for $4.59	2 lb for $1.89	4 lb for _____
3.	4 lb for $1.99	3 lb for $1.38	2 lb for $.90	1 lb for _____
4.	3 for $1.09	6 for $2.09	3 for $1.00	6 for _____
5.	3 for $4.59	4 for $6.40	2 for $3.09	5 for _____
6.	2 lb for $3.49	2 lb for $3.44	3 lb for $5.19	6 lb for _____

Using Probability Clues

Use before winter break.

Every number on the spinners below is a positive integer. On each
spinner, the number belonging to one sector is missing.

**Use the theoretical probability clues given to find each
missing number.**

1.

$P(\text{factor of } 27) = \frac{2}{3}$

$P(\text{prime number}) = \frac{1}{3}$

Missing number _____

2.

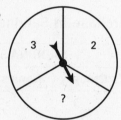

$P(\text{even number}) = \frac{2}{3}$

$P(\text{factor of } 6) = \frac{2}{3}$

$P(\text{number less than } 5) = 1$

Missing number _____

3.

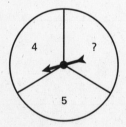

$P(\text{even}) = \frac{2}{3}$

$P(\text{factor of } 16) = \frac{2}{3}$

$P(\text{less than } 5) = \frac{1}{3}$

Missing number _____

4.

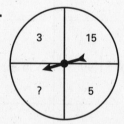

$P(\text{divisible by } 3) = \frac{3}{4}$

$P(\text{even number}) = 0$

$P(\text{between 6 and 10}) = \frac{1}{4}$

Missing number _____

5.

$P(\text{factor of } 24) = \frac{3}{4}$

$P(\text{even number}) = \frac{3}{4}$

$P(\text{between 5 and 8}) = \frac{3}{4}$

Missing number _____

6.

$P(\text{odd number}) = \frac{1}{5}$

$P(\text{multiple of } 9) = \frac{2}{5}$

$P(\text{less than } 30) = \frac{4}{5}$

Missing number _____

42 **Middle School Math, Course 3**
Special Activities Book

Name _____ Date _____

Draw the Triangle

Use before spring break.

**Try to draw an example of each triangle described below.
If it is impossible to draw the triangle, write *Not Possible*.
Then explain why.**

1. Right isosceles triangle

2. Right equilateral triangle

3. Right scalene triangle

4. Acute equilateral triangle

5. Obtuse equilateral triangle

6. Acute isosceles triangle

7. Obtuse isosceles triangle

8. Acute scalene triangle

Crack the Code

Use before spring break.

In each row, circle the formula in the row that is not equivalent to the others.

1.	area of parallelogram	**E.** $b + h$	**O.** bh	
2.	volume of rectangular prism	**L.** Bh	**P.** $\frac{1}{2}Bh$	
3.	circumference of circle	**D.** $2\pi r$	**R.** πr^2	
4.	volume of cylinder	**S.** $\pi r^2 h$	**N.** $2\pi r^2 h + 2\pi rh$	
5.	area of triangle	**O.** $\frac{1}{2}bh$	**A.** $\frac{1}{3}Bh$	
6.	volume of cone	**T.** $\pi r^2 h + \pi r\ell$	**U.** $\frac{1}{3}\pi r^2 h$	
7.	volume of pyramid	**E.** $\frac{1}{3}Bh$	**A.** $\frac{1}{2}Bh$	
8.	surface area of sphere	**G.** $\pi r^2 + \pi r\ell$	**W.** $4\pi r^2$	
9.	area of circle	**Z.** πr^2	**D.** $2\pi r$	
10.	perimeter of rectangle	**N.** $bh + bh$	**P.** $2\ell + 2w$	
11.	surface area of cylinder	**R.** $2\pi r^2 + 2\pi rh$	**W.** $\pi r^2 h$	
12.	surface area of cone	**N.** $\frac{1}{3}\pi r^2 h$	**R.** $\pi r^2 + \pi r\ell$	
13.	area of trapezoid	**Y.** $\frac{1}{2}bh$	**S.** $\frac{1}{2}(b_1 + b_2)h$	
14.	volume of sphere	**J.** $\pi r^2 h$	**Z.** $\frac{4}{3}\pi r^3$	
15.	area of rectangle	**C.** ℓw	**H.** $2\ell + 2w$	

Use your answers to Exercises 1–15 to answer the question. Write the letter of each circled answer in the space above each number.

Question: It is hard to believe that this simple and popular game was not invented until 1913. Its name did not appear in American dictionaries until 1930. What is it?

Answer: ___ ___ ___ ___ ___ ___ ___ ___ ___
   15 11   5   4 13   8   1 12   3

   ___ ___ ___ ___ ___ ___
   10   6   9 14   2   7

Name _____ **Date** _____

Number Puzzles

Use after Lesson 1.2.

Use any combination of the operations +, −, ×, or ÷, and any combination of the grouping symbols ( ), [ ], or fraction bars to write an expression that equals the number given. The first exercise shows one possible equation.

1. Use six 2s. Equals 14. $2 \times (2 + 2 + 2 + 2) - 2$ Equals 14

2. Use four 3s. Equals 7. _____

3. Use six 2s. Equals 13. _____

4. Use four 4s. Equals 3. _____

5. Use four 5s. Equals 2. _____

6. Use four 8s. Equals 1. _____

7. Use five 6s. Equals 3. _____

8. Use four 7s. Equals 14. _____

Name _____ **Date** _____

Number Patterns

Use after Lesson 1.3.

Look at the following patterns.

1, 6, 11, 16, 21, 26, . . .

Rule: $n + 5$

Create your own pattern.

1. Make up a number pattern involving addition. Start with 1 and write the first five numbers in your pattern. Ask a classmate to write the next five numbers and to write an algebraic expression that describes the pattern. (*Hint:* Let a variable represent the first number in the pattern.)

1, 3, 7, 15, 31, 63, . . .

Rule: $n \times 2 + 1$

2. Make up a number pattern involving addition *and* another operation. Start with 1 and write the first five numbers in your pattern. Have a classmate write the next five numbers and an algebraic expression that describes the pattern.

Solve the problem below.

3. One stormy night, Alexis invented a new substance with a volume of n liters. The mysterious substance quadrupled in size every day. Alexis stored it in a refrigerator with a capacity of $1000n$ liters. For how many days can Alexis safely leave her creation in the refrigerator if she starts with 1 liter?

Name _____ Date _____

Mystery Numbers

Use after Lesson 1.5.

The mystery number is located in the circle. Use the clues to find the value of the mystery number.

Puzzle 1: Find mystery number y.

$3y + 20 < 100$ and

$\dfrac{y}{2} > 10$

$y =$ _____

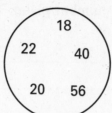

18
22   40
20   56

Puzzle 2: Find mystery number n.

$3n - 50 > 200$ and

$\dfrac{2n}{3} < 80$

$n =$ _____

44
58   126
84   160

Puzzle 3: Make up a mystery number puzzle like these for a classmate to solve. Use at least one variable in your clues.

CHAPTER 1

Name _____ Date _____

Equation Logic

Use after Lesson 1.7.

In the equations in the box, the six variables stand for the numbers 1, 2, 4, 6, 8, and 12. Examine the equations. Write the number each variable represents.

1. $a =$ _____

2. $b =$ _____

3. $c =$ _____

4. $d =$ _____

5. $e =$ _____

6. $f =$ _____

$$e = a + b$$
$$b = \dfrac{c}{e}$$
$$a = da$$
$$f = b + e$$
$$a = c - f$$

Discuss your reasoning with classmates.

Name _____ Date _____

Hidden Message

Use after Lesson 2.1.

Circle the integer in each row that meets the requirements for that row.

1. greater than -2	**B.** -3	**O.** -1	**F.** -12
2. less than -14	**E.** 15	**T.** -4	**I.** -15
3. opposite of 6	**U.** -12	**M.** -6	**R.** 0
4. absolute value of -8	**S.** -8	**M.** 0	**W.** 2^3
5. absolute value of 16	**U.** 8^2	**S.** -32	**N.** $(-2)^4$
6. less than -25	**D.** -10	**G.** -3^3	**A.** 6^2
7. greater than -8 but less than -2	**I.** 9	**E.** -2^4	**Y.** -5

Use your answers to Exercises 1–7 to answer the question below. Write the related letter in the space above each number.

Question: In 1924, which state became the first to elect a woman as governor?

Answer: ___ ___ ___ ___ ___ ___ ___
        4   7   1   3   2   5   6

Name _____ Date _____

Integer Squares

Use after Lesson 2.3.

Follow the directions below to complete each square.

To move one box to the right, add or subtract the integer shown by the horizontal arrow. To move one box up, add or subtract the integer shown by the vertical arrow.

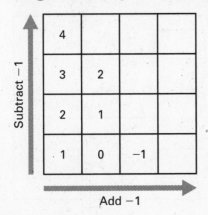

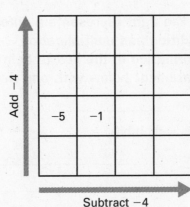

Name _____ Date _____

Means and Integers
Use after Lesson 2.5.

You can use integers to find the mean of a set of numbers. Study the example in the box for finding the mean of 84, 90, 91, 86, and 94.

Step 1: List the numbers in order from least to greatest.

Step 2: Select a number you think will be close to the mean. Choose 90 for this example.

Step 3: Write how far each number is from the mean you have chosen.

Step 4: Add the positive and negative integers:
$$-6 + (-4) + 0 + (+1) + (+4) = -5.$$

Step 5: Divide your sum by the number of addends:
$$-5 \div 5 = -1.$$

Step 6: Use the quotient to adjust your mean:
$$90 + (-1) = 89. \text{ The mean is 89.}$$

Distance from 90
$$84 \rightarrow -6$$
$$86 \rightarrow -4$$
$$90 \rightarrow 0$$
$$91 \rightarrow +1$$
$$94 \rightarrow +4$$

Use the method shown to find the mean for each number set.

1. 82, 81, 78, 85, 79

2. 58, 46, 55, 42, 49

3. 138, 141, 145, 142, 150, 148

4. 25, 36, 42, 18, 30, 24, 22, 35

Name _____ Date _____

Properties and Equations
Use after Lesson 2.7.

Each of the figures at the right represents a different whole number. Use addition and multiplication properties and the information in the box to help you complete each statement below with *one word*.

1. triangle + rectangle = _____

2. rectangle + (triangle + rhombus) = _____ + rhombus

3. rhombus × rectangle = _____

4. triangle + trapezoid = _____

5. circle − (triangle + rectangle) = _____

6. trapezoid × (rectangle + rhombus + triangle) = _____

Name _____ Date _____

Guess-and-Check Equations
Use after Lesson 3.2.

Use the integers from the box to complete the equations below. Use each integer only once.

6	5	4	3	2	1	0
−6	−5	−4	−3	−2	−1	

1. _____ + _____ = −11   **2.** _____ + _____ = −7

3. _____ + _____ = 9   **4.** _____ + _____ = 2

5. _____ + _____ = 7   **6.** _____ + _____ + _____ = 0

Challenge   Make up a "complete the equations" activity of your own.
Use both addition and subtraction. Ask a classmate to solve it.

Name _____ Date _____

Consecutive Integer Puzzles
Use after Lesson 3.4.

Consecutive integers are integers in counting order. −13, −12, and −11 are three consecutive integers. So are 4, 5, and 6. Consecutive *even* integers, such as −8 and −6, are two apart. So are consecutive *odd* integers, such as −1 and +1.

To find consecutive integers, you can write and solve two-step equations.

Think: Let n = the least integer.

To solve the problems below, choose a variable and write an equation.

1. Find two consecutive integers whose sum is −45.

2. Find three consecutive integers whose sum is 72.

3. Find two consecutive even integers whose sum is −34.

4. Find three consecutive even integers whose sum is −90.

5. Find three consecutive odd integers whose sum is −87.

6. Find four consecutive integers whose sum is 30.

7. Find four consecutive odd integers whose sum is −72.

8. Find five consecutive integers whose sum is 0.

Name _____ Date _____

Area and Perimeter Puzzles

Use after Lesson 3.5.

Use the information in the box to answer the questions below.
Hint: **Draw diagrams to help you visualize the squares.**

Each side of Square A measures 100 cm.

Square B has a perimeter of 100 cm.

The area of Square C is 100 cm^2.

Each side of Square D measures 4 m.

Square E has a perimeter of 4 m.

The area of Square F is 4 m^2.

---

1. Which square has the shortest sides?

2. Which square has the greatest perimeter?

3. Each side of which square is equal in length to the perimeter of Square E?

4. Which square would fit exactly four times into Square D?

5. Which square would fit exactly 100 times into Square A?

6. Which two squares are the same size?

Name _____ Date _____

Balance Scale Puzzle

Use after Lesson 3.7.

Read the problem below. Write the steps you would use to solve it. Compare your solution with those of your classmates.

Eight figurines are stolen from an art gallery. The police recover them all. In fact, they find nine. One is a fake. It looks and feels exactly like the others. However, it weighs slightly less than the others. The authorities have a balance scale they can use to find the fake figurine. How can they find the fake in *only two weighings*?

_____

_____

_____

_____

Name _____ Date _____

Greatest Common Factor

Use after Lesson 4.2.

Write the two numbers or expressions from each box that have the greatest common factor (GCF). Then write the GCF for those numbers or expressions.

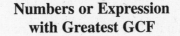

Numbers or Expression with Greatest GCF　　　**GCF**

1.

10	36	54
	25	48

_____　_____

2.

18	42	96
	27	72

_____　_____

3.

$36xy^2$	$54xy^2$	$126xy^2$
	$39xy^2$	$63xy^2$

_____　_____

Name _____ Date _____

Mystery Number

Use after Lesson 4.4.

Use the clues to find the mystery number.

1. I am a factor of 120. I am a multiple of 8 but not of 10.

What number am I? _____

2. I am the least common multiple (LCM) of two numbers whose sum is 27 and whose difference is 3.

What number am I? _____

3. I am the greatest common factor (GCF) of two numbers whose LCM is 30 and whose sum is 16.

What number am I? _____

4. I am the GCF of two numbers whose sum is 20 and whose difference is 4.

What number am I? _____

5. I am the LCM of three even numbers whose sum is 46. The largest of these numbers is 6 greater than the smallest.

What number am I? _____

6. I am the GCF of three numbers whose sum is 36. The smallest number is $\frac{1}{2}$ the largest. The middle number is the mean of the other two.

What number am I? _____

Name _____ Date _____

Forming Equivalent Fractions
Use after Lesson 4.5.

Use the numbers given to solve each problem. You may use a number more than once.

1. Use the numbers 2, 6, and 18 to form two fractions equivalent to $\frac{1}{3}$. _____

2. Use the numbers 3, 6, and 12 to form two fractions equivalent to $\frac{1}{2}$. _____

3. Use the numbers 9, 12, and 16 to form two fractions equivalent to $\frac{3}{4}$. _____

4. Use any whole number and the numbers 2 and 8 to form two fractions equivalent to $\frac{1}{4}$. _____

5. Use two whole numbers and the number 4 to form two fractions equivalent to $\frac{2}{3}$. _____

6. Make up a problem like those above. Solve the problem yourself first, then give it to a classmate to solve.

Name _____ Date _____

Exponents Game
Use after Lesson 4.7.

This game is for two players. You will need a spinner with ten sections numbered 0–9.

To play:

- Player 1 spins the spinner twice. The first number will be the base of an expression. The second number will be the negative exponent.

  Example: A spin of 3 and a spin of 5 become the expression 3^{-5}.

- Player 2 writes a multiplication expression and then a division expression, both having the first player's expression as an answer.

  Example: 3^{-5} can be written as $3^{-2} \times 3^{-3}$ and $3^{-8} \div 3^{-3}$.

- Player 1 checks the expressions written by Player 2. Each expression that results in a correct answer earns 1 point.

- Players switch roles. The first player to earn 10 points wins.

Name _____ **Date** _____

Fill in the Fractions

Use after Lesson 5.2.

Use the fractions in the figures to make each number sentence true.

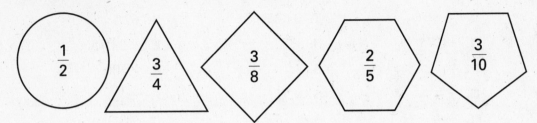

1. $\dfrac{9}{10} = $ _____ + _____

2. $1\dfrac{1}{5} = $ _____ + _____ + _____

3. $\dfrac{31}{40} = $ _____ + _____

4. $1\dfrac{5}{8} = $ _____ + _____ + _____

5. **Challenge** (*Hint:* Note the minus sign.) $\dfrac{13}{20} = $ _____ + _____ − _____

Name _____ **Date** _____

Using Mental Math

Use after Lesson 5.4.

Recall the distributive property: $a(b + c) = ab + ac$.

You can use this property to mentally find products involving mixed numbers.

> **Example:** $10 \times 1\dfrac{1}{2} = (10 \times 1) + \left(10 \times \dfrac{1}{2}\right)$
>
> $\qquad\qquad\quad = 10 + 5$
>
> $\qquad\qquad\quad = 15$

Use mental math to find each product.

1. $6 \times 1\dfrac{1}{2}$ 2. $2 \times 4\dfrac{1}{2}$ 3. $-12 \times 3\dfrac{1}{4}$

4. $-15 \times -2\dfrac{1}{5}$ 5. $-7 \times 3\dfrac{4}{7}$ 6. $-8 \times -6\dfrac{3}{4}$

7. $10 \times -5\dfrac{2}{5}$ 8. $30 \times 10\dfrac{2}{3}$ 9. $-9 \times 3\dfrac{2}{3}$

Name _____ Date _____

Crack the Code

Use after Lesson 5.6.

Circle the number in each row that is *not* equivalent.

1. **R.** 0.40   **A.** 0.4   **E.** 0.04   **B.** $\frac{2}{5}$

2. **R.** $\frac{25}{40}$ **D.** $\frac{5}{8}$ **T.** 0.625   **S.** 62.5

3. **P.** $-\frac{3}{4}$ **I.** -0.75 **O.** $-\frac{6}{8}$ **E.** -0.075

4. **T.** 1.6   **R.** $\frac{13}{5}$ **S.** $1\frac{3}{5}$ **R.** 1.600

5. **M.** -0.25 **N.** $-\frac{25}{100}$ **S.** 0.5^{-2} **P.** $-\frac{1}{4}$

6. **E.** $-3\frac{3}{10}$ **I.** $-\frac{33}{10}$ **A.** $-33\frac{1}{10}$ **O.** -3.3

7. **F.** $\left(\frac{1}{4}\right)^3$ **H.** $\frac{1}{64}$ **L.** 4^{-3} **K.** $\frac{1}{12}$

8. **T.** 0.0044   **N.** $\dfrac{44}{1000}$ **W.** $\dfrac{44}{10,000}$ **H.** $-4.4 \div -1000$

Use your answers to Exercises 1–8 to answer the following question. Write the related letter in the space above each exercise number below.

Question: These unique foot coverings with rubber soles were first introduced in 1917. They were brown and black. What do we call them today?

Answer: ____ ____ ____ ____ ____ ____ ____ ____
        5   8   1   6   7   3   4   2

Name _____ Date _____

The Mean Variation

Use after Lesson 5.8.

The *mean variation* measures the average distance from the mean.

To find the mean variation of a set of numbers:

• First, find the mean.	40, 50, 85, 90, 100	Mean = 73
• For each number in the data set, find the absolute value of the difference of the number and the mean.	$\begin{aligned}\lvert 73 - 40\rvert &= 33\\ \lvert 73 - 85\rvert &= 12\\ \lvert 73 - 100\rvert &= 27\end{aligned}$	$\begin{aligned}\lvert 73 - 50\rvert &= 23\\ \lvert 73 - 90\rvert &= 17\end{aligned}$
• Finally, find the mean of these differences.	33, 23, 12, 17, 27 = 112 ÷ 5 = 22.4	

Find the mean variation for each set of numbers.

1. 8, 35, 40, 7, 20 _____

2. 70, 60, 90, 95, 85, 50 _____

3. $-5, -8, -12, -6, -9, -2$ _____

4. 400, 375, 200, 120, 175, 320 _____

5. Why might the mean variation be a useful statistic? Explain.

Name _____ Date _____

Equivalent Equations

Use after Lesson 6.1.

**Use the property named to write an equivalent equation.
You do not have to solve the equation.**

Original Equation	Property	Equivalent Equation
1. $3(3 + n) = 15$	Distributive property	_____
2. $2n + 11 = 29$	Commutative property	_____
3. $(n + 7) + (-6) = 4$	Associative property	_____
4. $n(3 - 5) = 12$	Distributive property	_____
5. $4(-2 + n) = 5$	Distributive property	_____
6. $\dfrac{7n + 7}{7} = 14$	Distributive property	_____

Name _____ Date _____

Lengths of Segments

Use after Lesson 6.2.

In each figure below, $\overline{AB}$ and $\overline{CD}$ are the same length.

Find the length of each line segment below.

1.

A •———E——• B
$\quad 5x \qquad 4$

C •—————————• D
$\qquad 3(x + 6)$

2.

A •———E———• B
$\quad 7(n - 1) \quad 3n$

C •—————————• D
$\qquad 38$

3.

A •———E———• B
$\quad 3x \qquad 11$

C •—————————• D
$\qquad 5(x + 1)$

4.

A •—————————• B
$\qquad 39$

C •———E———• D
$\quad 4(n - 3) \quad 2n$

5.

A •—————————• B
$\qquad y + 11$

C •———E———• D
$\quad y + 4 \quad y + 9$

6.

A •———E——• B
$\quad w \quad 6w + 12$

C •—————————• D
$\qquad 2(w + 10)$

Name _____ Date _____

Circles in the Square

Use after Lesson 6.4.

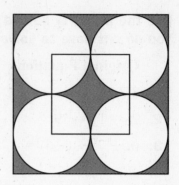

The diameter of each circle within the outer square is equal to half the length of the side of the square.

Use the information in the diagram to answer the questions.

1. Suppose the radius of each circle is 10 units. What is the area of the outer square? the inner square?

2. Suppose the radius of each circle is n units. What is the area of the outer square? the inner square?

3. Suppose the area of the outer square is 36 cm^2. What is the length of the radius of each circle?

4. Suppose the area of the inner square is 49 cm^2. What is the length of the radius of each circle?

Name _____ Date _____

Triangles and Inequalities

Use after Lesson 6.6.

In any triangle, the length of any one side is less than the sum of the lengths of the other two sides. You can use this information to write three inequalities.

Here are three inequalities that express the relationships between sides for the triangle below.

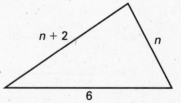

	one side	<	sum of other two sides
One Inequality	6	<	$n + (n + 2)$
Another Inequality	n	<	$6 + (n + 2)$
A Third Inequality	$n + 2$	<	$n + 6$

Simplify each inequality. Then answer the questions that follow.

1. $6 < n + (n + 2)$ 2. $n < 6 + (n + 2)$ 3. $n + 2 < n + 6$

4. Only one equivalent inequality tells you something about the value of n. What does it tell you?

5. Another triangle has sides of length x, 3, and 5. Use this information to write three inequalities. Then simplify each inequality. What can you say about the length of x?

Name _____ Date _____

On a Seesaw

Use after Lesson 7.2.

Two people can balance themselves on a seesaw by sitting the correct distances from the center, or fulcrum. The person who weighs more needs to sit closer to the fulcrum.

You can express the two weights and distances from the fulcrum when the seesaw is balanced by using this proportion: $\dfrac{W_1}{W_2} = \dfrac{d_2}{d_1}$

- W_1 = the weight of the first person
- d_2 = the distance the second person sits from the fulcrum
- W_2 = the weight of the second person
- d_1 = the distance the first person sits from the fulcrum

Use the above proportion to solve each seesaw problem.

1. Pablo weighs 60 kg and Elena weighs 40 kg. If Elena sits 360 cm from the fulcrum, how far from it must Pablo sit to balance the seesaw?

2. Mori weighs 45 kg and sits 450 cm from the fulcrum of a seesaw. The seesaw is balanced, if Candi sits 750 cm from the fulcrum. How much does Candi weigh?

3. *Challenge* Gita weighs 35 kg and sits 200 cm from the fulcrum of a seesaw. Maya, her little sister, weighs 15 kg and sits 350 cm from the fulcrum on the other side. How much more weight does Maya need on her end of the seesaw to make it balance?

Name _____ Date _____

Unreasonable Claims

Use after Lesson 7.4.

The following ads and headlines needs a better proofreader. Many of the ads and headlines do not make sense, while others contain errors. Circle the ads and headlines that make unreasonable claims or contain mistakes. Explain your thinking.

1. The prices of all coats are reduced by 110%! Don't wait!

2. Five out of eight, or 70%, of our customers are repeat customers.

3. LaSalle Lions Football Slumping! They have lost 80% of their games this month.

4. Luke's Loans offers a special one-time-only low, low annual interest rate of 82.5%!!

5. Jose Hernandez, with 20 hits out of 50 at-bats, has a league-leading batting average of 0.600.

6. Fern's Family Restaurant now charges a 35% tip for all large groups.

7. Buy FreshMouth toothpaste. 98% of all dentists surveyed said it was their first choice for fighting tooth decay.

8. A burger/shake/fry combo at Snack Shack provides 2% of the Surgeon General's recommended daily calorie intake.

Name _____ Date _____

Shopping for Rugs
Use after Lesson 7.6.

At Ray's Rug Outlet, all rugs and carpets are initially sold at a discount of 10% off the manufacturer's suggested list price. Ray slashes prices further in the following manner:

- reduces price by an additional 20% off after 1 week in the store
- reduces price by an additional 25% off after 2 weeks in the store
- reduces price by an additional 50% off after 3 weeks in the store

Use Ray's pricing system to solve each problem.

1. A rug has been at Ray's for 9 days. What is Ray's price for it, if the manufacturer listed it at $100?

2. A carpet's list price is $500. Rosa buys it from Ray after it has been in the store for 15 days. What does she pay?

3. Mike's parents bought a carpet that had been at Ray's for a month. Its list price was $1650. What did they pay?

4. Hiram bought a rug that had been in the store for 10 days. He paid $57.60 for it. What was its suggested list price?

5. Make up a problem of your own using Ray's pricing system. Solve it yourself before presenting it to others.

CHAPTER
7

Name _____ Date _____

Describing Probabilities
Use after Lesson 7.7.

Cards can be drawn at random from a standard 52-card deck. Recall that a deck of cards has four suits: Hearts, Diamonds, Clubs, and Spades. Each suit has the following cards: 2, 3, 4, 5, 6, 7, 8, 9, 10, Jack, Queen, King, and Ace. The Diamonds and Hearts are red. The Spades and Clubs are black. Use the probability table. Write the condition that describes each probability.

Probability Table	
Condition	**Probability**
certain	1.00
very likely	0.75–0.99
likely	0.51–0.74
fifty-fifty	0.50
unlikely	0.25–0.49
very unlikely	0.01–0.24
impossible	0.00

1. A black 4 is drawn.   very unlikely

2. A club or a spade is drawn.   _____

3. A red card greater than a 3 is drawn.   _____

4. A card greater than a 3 is drawn.   _____

5. A heart, a diamond, a spade, or a club is drawn.   _____

6. A 14 of diamonds is drawn.   _____

Name _____ Date _____

8 Estimating Angle Measures

Use after Lesson 8.1.

Play an angle estimation game with a partner.

To play, estimate the angle measures. Record your estimates. Then use a protractor to find the actual measurements. For each angle, the player whose estimate comes the closest wins a point.

1.    **2.**   **3.**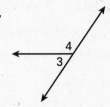

4. Continue this game by constructing your own angles for other pairs of players to estimate. Include vertical angles as well as angles formed by lines transversing sets of parallel lines.

CHAPTER

Name _____ Date _____

8 Draw the Figure

Use after Lesson 8.4.

Sketch each figure. If it is impossible to do so, write
***Not Possible*, and explain why.**

1. a rectangle with congruent sides	**2.** a trapezoid with no right angles
3. an acute scalene triangle	**4.** a triangle with two obtuse angles
5. a quadrilateral with exactly two right angles	**6.** a trapezoid with two congruent sides
7. a polygon with exactly three diagonals	**8.** a pentagon with two right angles
9. a quadrilateral with congruent diagonals	**10.** an obtuse equilateral triangle

Name _____ Date _____

Make and Use Equilateral Triangles

Use after Lesson 8.5.

Materials: compass, straightedge, scissors

You can use a compass and a straightedge to make an equilateral triangle. Follow the steps to make triangle ABC.

- Draw and label $\overline{AB}$ to be 6 cm long.

- With your compass still opened to 6 cm, place one end on point A. Draw an arc above $\overline{AB}$.

- With your compass still opened to 6 cm, place one end on point B. Draw another arc above $\overline{AB}$.

- Label the point where the arcs intersect as point C.

- Use your straightedge to draw $\overline{AC}$ and $\overline{BC}$.

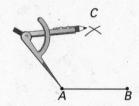

Figures made by fitting two or more equilateral triangles together are called *polyiamonds*. Using two equilateral triangles, you can form the simplest polyiamond—a diamond.

Construct and cut out 6 equilateral triangles. Find how many polyiamonds you can make using these triangles. *Hint:* Sketch each one on graph paper to keep track and avoid duplications.

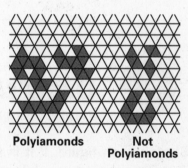

Polyiamonds   Not Polyiamonds

Name _____ Date _____

Symmetrical Letters

Use after Lesson 8.6.

Some capital letters, such as C and D, are symmetrical about a horizontal line. Others, such as A and T, are symmetrical about a vertical line.

Work with a partner. First, list all the capital letters that are symmetrical about a horizontal line. Then use those letters to write words, phrases, or sentences containing only those letters. Repeat this exercise, this time using only letters that are symmetrical about a vertical line.

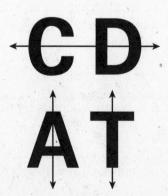

When you have finished, swap your efforts with other pairs of students. Who wrote the most elaborate phrase? the most creative? the most humorous?

Name _____ Date _____

Crack the Code

Use after Lesson 9.2.

Circle the irrational number in each row.

1.   I. $4.\overline{3}$ E. π A. $\sqrt{9}$

2.   U. $\sqrt{100}$ N. 0 M. $2.3456\ldots$

3.   S. -12.4 R. $1.21314151\ldots$ T. $5.46\overline{8}$

4.   P. $\sqrt{2}$ D. $-3\frac{4}{5}$ F. $2.2222\ldots$

5.   U. $\sqrt{49}$ L. 3 T. $6.707007000\ldots$

6.   O. 0.003003003 U. $\sqrt{43}$ A. $16.\overline{6}$

7.   R. -11.305 T. $-4.81881811\ldots$ W. $5\frac{1}{7}$

Use your answers to Exercises 1–7 to answer the question below.

Question: The first musical instrument was probably made from a hollow bamboo cane or eucalyptus branch. The first metal one was silver and was discovered in the tomb of the Egyptian king Tutankhamen. What instrument is it?

Answer: ____ ____ ____ ____ ____ ____ ____
       5   3   6   2   4   1   7

Name _____ Date _____

Investigating Triangles

Use after Lesson 9.3.

Materials: protractor, straightedge

You know that when the side lengths a, b, and c of a triangle satisfy the Pythagorean theorem $(a^2 + b^2 = c^2)$, the triangle is a right triangle.

But what can you say about a triangle when $a^2 + b^2 < c^2$?

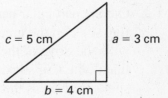

$c = 5$ cm $a = 3$ cm $b = 4$ cm

1. Use the triangle shown to help you think about this question. Draw a triangle with $a = 3$ cm, $b = 4$ cm, and $c = 6$ cm. Substitute the values of this triangle into the inequality $a^2 + b^2 < c^2$. What kind of triangle satisfies $a^2 + b^2 < c^2$? Explain. (*Hint:* What happens to the right angle?)

2. What kind of triangle satisfies the inequality $a^2 + b^2 > c^2$? Explain.

CHAPTER 9

Name _____ Date _____

Pythagorean Triples

Use after Lesson 9.5.

A Pythagorean triple is a set of three positive integers, a, b, and c, such that $a^2 + b^2 = c^2$. For example, $3^2 + 4^2 = 5^2$. So, the numbers 3, 4, and 5 are a Pythagorean triple.

The table shows an algebraic method for finding Pythagorean triples. Substitute any value for m and simplify each expression. Then check to see if the set is a Pythagorean triple. Use this method to find ten sets of Pythagorean triples.

	a^2	b^2	c^2	Check
	$2m$	$m^2 - 1$	$m^2 + 1$	$a^2 + b^2 = c^2$
$m = 3$	$2 \times 3 = 6$	$(3 \times 3) - 1 = 8$	$(3 \times 3) + 1 = 10$	$6^2 + 8^2 = 10^2$ $36 + 64 = 100$ $100 = 100$

CHAPTER 9

Name _____ Date _____

Choosing the Right Ratio

Use after Lesson 9.6.

Read each problem carefully but do not solve it. Instead, draw and label a sketch of it. Then write the trigonometric ratio you would use to find the missing information. Be prepared to explain your decisions.

1. On one particular par-3 golf hole, the distance from the tee to the flag stick on the green is 150 yards. A golfer tees off. The golfer pulls the drive of the ball to the left at an angle of 14° from a direct line to the flag stick. His ball ends up directly to the left of the flag stick. How far is the ball from the flag stick on the green?

2. Ralph is painting his house. He rests his 8 foot ladder against a side of the house at an angle of 69° from the horizontal. How far from the house has he placed the ladder?

3. A crow sits atop a telephone pole that is 25 feet high. The crow spots dinner on the ground and dives down toward it at an angle of 20° with the horizontal. How long is the crow's flight?

Name _____ Date _____

Area of a Rhombus

Use after Lesson 10.1.

A rhombus is a parallelogram with four sides of equal length. The formula $A = bh$ is used to find the area of any parallelogram. However, there is a special formula you can use to find the area of a rhombus. Examine the picture and answer the questions that follow to develop a formula for the area of a rhombus.

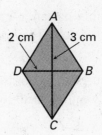
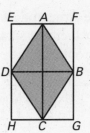

The first figure shows rhombus $ABCD$ with perpendicular diagonals of lengths 2 cm and 3 cm. Rectangle $EFGH$ has sides parallel to the diagonals of the rhombus.

1. Look at the drawings. How does the length of base $\overline{GH}$ of rectangle $EFGH$ compare with the length of diagonal $\overline{DB}$? How does the height of rectangle $EFGH$ compare with diagonal $\overline{AC}$?

2. Use the formula $A = bh$ to find the area of rectangle $EFGH$.

3. What fractional part of the rectangle does the rhombus cover?

4. Name the diagonals of the rhombus d_1 and d_2. Using the labels d_1 and d_2, write a formula for the area of rhombus $ABCD$.

5. What is the area of rhombus $ABCD$?

Name _____ Date _____

Word Scramble

Use after Lesson 10.3.

Use the context clues to unscramble the words.

1. A *ditazordep* is a quadrilateral with exactly one pair of parallel sides.

   _____

2. A chord passing through the center of a circle is called a *eamdrtie*.

   _____

3. A solid enclosed by polygons is a *nodrelhopy*.

   _____

4. A polyhedron with one base is a *drimapy*.

   _____

5. A *drinecly* is a solid figure with two congruent circular bases that lie in parallel planes.

   _____

6. The bases of a *gauntirlar smirp* are congruent triangles.

   _____

7. A *enco* is a solid with one circular base.

   _____

8. To find the area of a *lorglapramela*, multiply the base by the height.

   _____

Name _____ Date _____

Painting the Pool

Use after Lesson 10.4.

The Armstrong family has an in-ground swimming pool, the dimensions of which are shown below. They plan to paint the entire pool but not the surrounding area.

1. What is the surface area of the swimming pool? Explain how you obtained your answer.

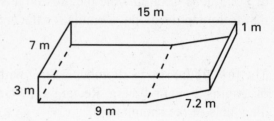

2. Each can of paint the Armstrongs will use covers 20 m². How many cans of paint will they need?

Name _____ Date _____

Drawing Diagrams

Use after Lesson 10.6.

Draw a diagram to help you solve each problem.

1. A square has the same number of centimeters in its perimeter as it has square centimeters in its area. What is the length of a side of the square?

2. A circle has the same number of inches in its circumference as there are square inches in its area. What is the length of its diameter?

3. Ms. Perez owns a square piece of property that measures 100 meters on a side. She is giving parts of it away to her three grandchildren. She will give Martin a lot that has an area of 3600 m². For herself, she plans to keep an area of 1600 m². She will give same-sized lots to each of her other grandchildren. What is the size of each of these last two lots?

4. A square piece of cardboard has 10 inch sides. It will be made into an open box by cutting from each corner equal-sized squares. Then the sides will be folded up and taped. Which box will have the greater volume: a box made by cutting 1 inch squares out of the corners or a box made by cutting 2 inch squares out of the corners? How much greater will that volume be?

Name _____ Date _____

When is a Pi Not a Pi?

Use after Lesson 11.2.

Genji measured the diameters of
several cylinders and compared it
to the circumferences of their bases.
His results are shown at the right.

Diameter (*d*)	0.5	1	1.5	2	2.5	3
Circumference (*C*)	1.5	3	4.75	6.25	8	9.5

1. Use Genji's results to make a scatter plot at the right. Using a ruler, draw a line passing through as many of the points as possible.

2. Using your scatter plot, suggest a rule that best represents your results. Does your rule match any of the data pairs? Does it match all of them?

3. Did Genji prove that π is a number other than 3.14159 . . .? Why or why not?

Name _____ Date _____

The Midpoint Formula

Use after Lesson 11.4.

You can use a formula to find the coordinates of the midpoint of
a line segment in a coordinate plane. To do this, find the mean of the
x-coordinates of the endpoints (x_1 and x_2), and then find the mean of
the *y*-coordinates of the endpoints (y_1 and y_2).

$$\text{Midpoint Formula} = \left(\frac{x_1 + x_2}{2}, \frac{y_1 + y_2}{2}\right)$$

Find the midpoint of $\overline{QR}$. Endpoint Q is located at $(-3, 2)$. Endpoint R is located at $(7, -2)$.

$$\left(\frac{-3 + 7}{2}, \frac{2 + (-2)}{2}\right) = \left(\frac{4}{2}, \frac{0}{2}\right) = (2, 0)$$

The midpoint is located at $(2, 0)$.

Write the coordinates of the midpoint of each line segment.

1. $A(-3, -5)$, $B(7, -5)$

2. $M(0, 5)$, $N(-6, -8)$

3.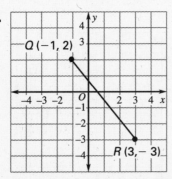

4.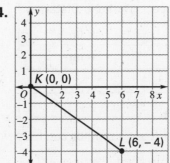

Name _____ Date _____

Slopes and Squares

Use after Lesson 11.6.

The slopes of parallel lines and perpendicular lines have special properties:

• Parallel lines have the same slope.

• Perpendicular lines have slopes that are negative reciprocals.

For example, think about a segment that has a slope of $\frac{1}{3}$. This means that from any point on the line you can move over 3 and up 1 to find another point on the line.

The perpendicular line will have a slope of $-\frac{3}{1}$. So from any point on this line, you can move over 1 and down 3 OR back 1 and up 3.

Use the slope of each segment to draw a square that has the given segment as one side. Then name the vertices of the square.

1. 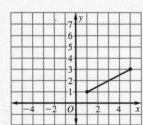   **2.** 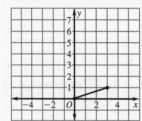   **3.**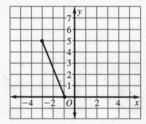

Name _____ Date _____

Playing Catch-up

Use after Lesson 11.7.

Solve the problem by filling in a table and making a line graph.

Rosa left her house at 4 P.M., driving at a constant speed of 30 mi/h. Her mother left the same house at 6 P.M., driving in the same direction at a constant speed of 45 mi/h.

Extend and complete a table similar to this one.

Graph Rosa's travel and her mother's travel. Label each line.

Time	Rosa's Distance	Mother's Distance
4:00	0 mi	0 mi
5:00	30 mi	0 mi
6:00		

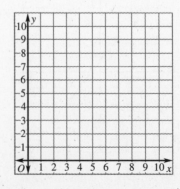

1. At what time did Rosa's mother catch up with her?

2. How does the table show the answer?

3. How does the graph show the answer?

Name _____ Date _____

Using a Stem-and-Leaf Plot

Use after Lesson 12.2.

Complete the following activity in which you collect data. Make a stem-and-leaf plot to display your findings. Conclude by interpreting your findings.

- Use a centimeter ruler or a tape measure to find the height, in centimeters, of each of your classmates. Work together to gather and share this data.

- Make a stem-and-leaf plot to display your findings.

- Find and record the range, mean, median, and mode of the data.

- Write a summary of what your plot shows about the heights of your classmates.

Challenge Now make a box-and-whisker plot of the same data. Compare and contrast your two data displays.

Name _____ Date _____

Two Different Impressions

Use after Lesson 12.3.

The table shows the average hourly wages of employees at CD World. Use the data in the table and follow each step below.

Year	1999	2000	2001	2002	2003
Average Hourly Wage	$10.00	$10.50	$11.00	$11.50	$12.00

You can vary the impression a line graph creates by changing the scale you use.

1. Make two different line graphs to display the data in the table.

   (a) Make one graph from the standpoint of the employees of the store, who want to communicate that wages are rising too slowly.

   (b) Make another graph from the standpoint of the owner of the store, who wants to communicate that wages are rising too quickly.

2. Examine and compare your two graphs. Explain the differences you see. Which graph is correct? Explain.

3. Suppose you are the owner of CD World and you would like to display the same data in a bar graph. Construct a bar graph that gives the impression that employee wages have been rising too rapidly.

CHAPTER 12

Name _____ Date _____

Permutations and Combinations

Use after Lesson 12.6.

Follow the steps to discover an interesting shortcut for finding some combinations.

Remember in combination notation $(_nC_r)$, n represents the number of objects, and r represents the number of objects taken at a time.

1. Find the values of $_5C_3$ and $_5C_2$. What do you notice?

2. Find the values of $_8C_6$ and $_8C_2$. Again, what do you notice?

3. Now add the number of objects taken at a time for $_5C_3$ to the number of objects taken at a time for $_5C_2$. Then do the same for $_8C_6$ and $_8C_2$. Compare each sum with the total number of objects for each combination. What do you notice about the two sums?

4. Does this pattern work for other combinations? Find out using $_{12}C_{10}$ and $_{12}C_2$. Then try $_{20}C_{16}$ and $_{20}C_4$.

5. Use this pattern and the shortcut it provides to find $_{47}C_{45}$. How did you do it?

CHAPTER 12

Name _____ Date _____

Crack the Code

Use after Lesson 12.7.

Circle each expression in row 1–9 at the right that is *not* equivalent to the others.

	Probability	Odds	Probability	Odds
1.	**C.** $\frac{2}{5}$	**D.** $2:3$	**A.** $\frac{2}{3}$	**R.** $4:6$
2.	**E.** $\frac{3}{8}$	**A.** $3:5$	**I.** $\frac{6}{16}$	**O.** $8:3$
3.	**O.** $\frac{8}{14}$	**E.** $4:11$	**A.** $\frac{4}{7}$	**T.** $4:3$
4.	**H.** $\frac{6}{16}$	**S.** $5:4$	**R.** $\frac{5}{9}$	**F.** $10:8$
5.	**D.** $\frac{1}{6}$	**W.** $1:5$	**P.** $\frac{2}{12}$	**C.** $1:7$
6.	**T.** $\frac{7}{8}$	**L.** $8:7$	**U.** $\frac{21}{24}$	**I.** $7:1$
7.	**O.** $\frac{2}{3}$	**E.** $2:4$	**A.** $\frac{1}{3}$	**S.** $1:2$
8.	**J.** $\frac{1}{2}$	**G.** $1:1$	**L.** $\frac{5}{10}$	**C.** $2:1$
9.	**R.** $\frac{1}{10}$	**T.** $1:11$	**P.** $\frac{2}{20}$	**B.** $1:9$

Use your answers to Exercises 1–9 to fill in the blanks below and answer the question. Write the letter of the answer you circled in the space above each exercise number below.

Question: Three thousand years ago, this food was a bitter ceremonial brew favored by Native American civilizations. It is a sweet treat today. What is it?

Answer: ___ ___ ___ ___ ___ ___ ___ ___ ___
           8   4   7   5   2   6   1   9   3

Name _____ Date _____

Polynomial Code

Use after Lesson 13.1.

Circle the polynomial in each row that is *not* written in standard form.

1. C. $3x^3 + 2x$ D. $x^4 + 3x^3 - 2x$ P. $4x^3 + x + 3x^2$ R. $2x^3 + 3x^2 - 2x$

2. E. $4x^2 + x + 3x^4$ A. $3x^3 + 2x$ I. $3x^3 + 2x$ O. $3x^3 + 2^4$

3. B. $x^4 + 3x^2 - 2x$ F. $x^2 - 3x^3 + 2^4$ A. $x^4 + 3x^2 - 2x$ T. $5x^4 + 3x^3 - 2x$

4. H. $x^3 - 3x^2 - x$ S. $x^4 + 8x^3 - 12x$ R. $x^4 - x^3 - x$ O. $x^3 + 3x + 2x^2$

5. D. $8x^4 + 3x^3 - 2x$ W. $x^4 + x^3 + 3$ O. $x^3 + 3 + 4x^4$ P. $x^4 + 3x^3 - 2x + 5$

6. T. $x^3 - 3 + 4x^2$ L. $x^5 + 3x^4 - 9x$ U. $2x^3 + 8x^2 - x$ I. $x^3 + 3x^2 - 6$

7. O. $x^4 + x^3 - x$ T. $2x^4 - x^3 - 5x$ E. $4x^4 - 3^2 + 4x^2$ S. $13x^4 + 13x^3 - 13x^2$

8. F. $x + 3 + 4x^2$ G. $6x^6 + 3x^3 + 2$ L. $4x^4 + x^3 - 5x$ C. $3x^3 - 2x$

9. R. $x^4 + 8x^3 - x$ T. $4x^4 - 4x^3 - 4x$ P. $x^4 + 18x^3 - 5x^2$ C. $x - 2x^2$

Use your answers to Exercises 1–9 to fill in the blanks below and answer the question. Write the letter of the answer you circled in the space above each exercise number below.

Question: This welcome kitchen accessory was created by a French pharmacist 200 years ago. What is it?

Answer: ____ ____ ____ ____ ____ ____ ____ ____ ____
       9   5   8   3   7   2   1   4   6

Name _____ Date _____

Problems and Answers

Use after Lesson 13.4.

Look at each diagram. Write the multiplication problem and the answer it illustrates.

1.
	x	5
$2x$	$2x^2$	$10x$
1	x	5

2.
	y	8
$3y$	$3y^2$	$24y$
2	$2y$	16

3.
	$4x$	3
x^2	$4x^3$	$3x^2$
$6x$	$24x^2$	$18x$

4.
	y^2	4
y^3	y^5	$4y^3$
$-4y$	$-4y^3$	$-16y$

Is it Magic?

Use after Lesson 13.5.

Try the following activity.

- Write a set of three consecutive integers. (Remember, consecutive integers are integers in counting order, such as 4, 5, and 6.)

- Multiply the first of the three numbers by the last number. Square the middle number. What happens?

- Try this procedure with 6 more sets of three consecutive integers. What do you notice?

- Use algebraic reasoning and your understanding of multiplying binomials to explain why this will always happen. *Hint:* Let x represent the first number, let $x + 1$ stand for the second number, and let $x + 2$ stand for the third number in each set.

Share your findings with your classmates.

_____

Graph the Path

Use after Lesson 13.6.

Read the story below. On centimeter graph paper, show the ladybug's path. Use the equation to graph the path the ladybug makes through the first quadrant.

A ladybug is standing at the origin of a coordinate grid. It then crawls its way through Quadrant I in a path that can be described by the following equation:

$$y = x - \frac{x^2}{8}$$

Then, when the ladybug reaches the x-axis again, it stops.

Answer each question.

1. What are the coordinates of the point at which the ladybug begins its journey?

2. What are the coordinates of the point on the x-axis where the ladybug stops?

3. How many centimeters high does the ladybug go in the first quadrant?

4. How many centimeters away from its starting point does the ladybug go?

Answers to Start of School Activities

Start of School

Make the Numbers

1. 976,531. **2.** .135679 **3.** 39.7651

4. 513.679 **5.** .796531 **6.** .379651

7. 6351.79 **8.** 675.931 **9.** .651379

10. .569731 **11.** 9.75136 **12.** 3.15796

Consecutive Integers

1. $-13, -12$ **2.** 23, 24, 25

3. $-12, -11, -10$ **4.** $-24, -22$

5. $-32, -30, -28$ **6.** 18, 19, 20, 21

7. $-31, -29, -27$ **8.** $-2, -1, 0, 1, 2$

Use the Properties

1. $12 + 6$ **2.** $(3 + 7)3$ **3.** $6n + 30$

4. $3 + x$ **5.** $n + (4 + 6)$ **6.** $3y + 36$

7. $(2 \times 5)n$ **8.** $5 + 9x$

9. associative property of addition

10. commutative property of addition

11. distributive property **12.** distributive property **13.** associative property of multiplication **14.** commutative property of multiplication **15.** distributive property

16. 223

Crack the Code

LAWNMOWER

Form the Fractions

1. $\frac{2}{6}; \frac{6}{18}$ **2.** $\frac{1}{5}; \frac{5}{25}$ **3.** $\frac{3}{6}; \frac{6}{12}$ **4.** $\frac{9}{12}; \frac{12}{16}$

5. $\frac{2}{8}; \frac{8}{32}$ **6.** $\frac{3}{15}; \frac{15}{75}$ **7.** possible answer: $\frac{4}{6}$ and $\frac{6}{9}$

Parts of a Whole

1. $\frac{1}{2}$ **2.** $\frac{1}{4}$ **3.** $\frac{1}{12}$ **4.** $\frac{1}{12}$ **5.** $\frac{1}{12}$ **6.** $\frac{1}{48}$

7. $\frac{5}{12}$ **8.** 0 **9.** $\frac{5}{144}$ **10.** $\frac{3}{16}$ **11.** 4 **12.** 2

Crossnumber Puzzle

¹1	²2	³5	■	⁴4	⁵0	■	⁶1	0	■	⁷8	⁸2
■	⁹6	2	¹⁰5	■	¹¹0	4	5	■	¹²1	0	■
¹³9	■	¹⁴2	2	¹⁵5	■	■	¹⁶2	8	■	■	■
¹⁷0	¹⁸0	¹⁹7	■	0	■	²⁰8	7	5	■	²²4	²³2
■	²⁴1	0	5	■	²⁵3	7	5	■	²⁶1	5	0

Geometric Word Search

S	C	O	N	E	Y	—	A	X	I	S
O	T	R	O	D	I	M	A	R	Y	P
L	E	L	L	A	R	A	P	J	N	R
I	B	Y	E	C	U	B	E	P	I	E
D	I	A	G	O	N	A	L	L	I	L
T	P	R	I	S	M	L	G	A	D	G
C	O	C	T	A	G	O	N	N	A	N
E	L	A	C	S	A	Z	A	E	R	A
S	L	E	L	C	R	I	C	D	O	K
I	R	T	E	T	N	E	M	G	E	S
B	A	R	C	X	E	T	R	E	V	U

Line Segment Puzzles

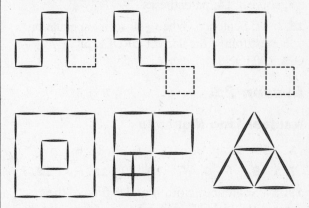

Coordinate Plane Puzzlers

1. $(6, -2)$ **2.** $(0, 3)$ **3.** $(0, -2)$ **4.** $(6, 0.5)$

5. 60 square units **6.** $(-4, 4), (4, 6), (4, -4)$

7. $(3, 6), (-1, -2), (11, 2)$

8. a. I **b.** III **c.** IV **d.** II

Answers to Activities for Substitutes

Lesson 1.4

Coded Alphabet-Substitution Message

1. 5 **2.** 22 **3.** 1 **4.** 12 **5.** 21 **6.** 1 **7.** 20
8. 5 **9.** 16 **10.** 15 **11.** 23 **12.** 5 **13.** 18
14. 19; Statement: To follow the correct order of operations, first compute inside the parentheses, then EVALUATE POWERS before multiplying in order from left to right. **15–19.** Check students' work.; Statement: 10^3 has THREE zeros.

Lesson 1.7

Hidden Words Puzzle

1. histogram **2.** variable **3.** data
4. frequency **5.** expressions **6.** solution
7. exponent **8.** area **9.** bar graph
10. evaluate **11.** equation **12.** perimeter
13. solve **14.** parentheses

15. base; Sentence: When you solve an equation, you must follow the correct ORDER of OPERATIONS.

Lesson 2.5

Number Line Message

1. -10 **2.** 4 **3.** -9 **4.** 0 **5.** 8 **6.** -5
7. 5 **8.** -6 **9.** -7 **10.** -2 **11.** -4 **12.** 7
13. 2 Sentence: Both 6 and -6 have the same ABSOLUTE VALUE.
14–20. Answers will vary.

Lesson 2.8

Coordinate Message

The four sets of coordinates spell out: MATH.
2. Answers will vary.

Lesson 3.4

Hidden Message

1. $a = 13$ **2.** $e = -3$ **3.** $e = 0$ **4.** $e = 10$
5. $i = -10$ **6.** $i = 20$ **7.** $n = -5.5$
8. $n = 25$ **9.** $o = 22$ **10.** $o = 1$ **11.** $p = 5.5$
12. $r = -2.4$ **13.** $r = 12.6$ **14.** $s = -1.8$
15. $s = 30$ **16.** $t = 15.5$

17. $v = -4.2$; Sentence: To undo operations, use INVERSE OPERATIONS.

Lesson 3.7

Hidden Words Puzzle

1. inverse **2.** inequality **3.** solution **4.** height
5. value **6.** base **7.** simplify **8.** negative
9. length **10.** multiply **11.** yes **12.** equals
13. subtract **14.** add **15.** substitute **16.** thirty
17. solve **18.** ninety **19.** six; Sentence: When the values of the variables of two equations are always the same, then they are EQUIVALENT EQUATIONS.

Lesson 4.4

Coded Message

1. 2 **2.** 15 **3.** $2\frac{1}{2}$ **4.** $26\frac{3}{4}$ **5.** $\frac{4}{5}$
6. 40 **7.** 7 **8.** 30 **9.** $11\frac{1}{5}$
10. Any fraction equivalent to $\frac{1}{2}$ is acceptable.
11. 97 **12.** 11 **13.** 25 **14.** 1 **15.** 36
16. 20 **17.** $1\frac{1}{4}$ **18.** 76 **19.** 3

Statement: The LEAST COMMON MULTIPLE of two numbers is the least number that is a common multiple of both of them.

Lesson 4.8

Hidden Term

1. GCF **2.** prime **3.** eleven **4.** relatively
5. multiples **6.** numerical **7.** least **8.** forty
9. factors **10.** monomial **11.** simplest
12. composite **13.** one **14.** scientific
Statement: Eleven is the GREATEST COMMON factor of 121 and 132.

Lesson 5.4

Matching Expressions

1. D **2.** I **3.** V **4.** I **5.** D **6.** I **7.** N
8. G **9.** U **10.** S **11.** E **12.** T **13.** H
14. E **15.** R **16.** E **17.** C **18.** I **19.** P
20. R **21.** O **22.** C **23.** A **24.** L
Message: Dividing? Use the reciprocal!

Answers to Activities for Substitutes *continued*

Lesson 5.8 *(Sample Answers)*

Box Scores

1. $3.16 + (-1.845)$ **2.** $3 \cdot 2.6$ **3.** $12 \div \frac{1}{3}$
4. $(-6.49) - \left(-6\frac{1}{2}\right)$ **5.** $-6\frac{1}{2}, -6.49, -1.845,$
$\frac{1}{3}, 2.6, 3, 3.16, 12$ **6.** 1.46 **7.** 0.78 **8.** 18.5
9. $\frac{1}{3}$ **10–13.** Answers will vary.

Lesson 6.3

Matching Code

1. C **2.** O **3.** M **4.** B **5.** I **6.** N **7.** E
8. L **9.** I **10.** K **11.** E **12.** T **13.** E
14. R **15.** M **16.** S

Statement: The first step in simplifying an expression or equation is to COMBINE LIKE TERMS.

Lesson 6.6

Figure a Message

1. S **2.** U **3.** B **4.** S **5.** T **6.** I
7. T **8.** U **9.** T **10.** E

Statement: To find the value of an expression, SUBSTITUTE a value for each variable.

Statement: To undo multiplication, DIVIDE.

Lesson 7.4

Coded Message

1. 50 ft **2.** 3 oz **3.** $\frac{1}{2}$ ft **4.** 65 mi **5.** 70 h
6. 3 qt **7.** 70 mi **8.** 20 min **9.** $\frac{1}{2}$ mi
10. 3 gal **11.** \$20 **12.** \$140

First statement: The CROSS PRODUCTS ARE EQUAL.

Lesson 7.8

Word Maze

1. ratio **2.** outcome **3.** equivalent **4.** three
5. rate **6.** numerator **7.** *across:* proportion
7. *down:* percent **8.** theoretical **9.** liters
10. scale **11.** eight **12.** discount **13.** second
14. *across:* increase **14.** *down:* inch **15.** hand
16. decrease **17.** event **18.** twenty

Lesson 8.4

Missing Angles

1. 105° **2.** 75° **3.** 115° **4.** 65° **5.** 145°
6. 35° **7.** 155° **8.** 25°

Statement: In a right triangle, the two acute angles are COMPLEMENTARY.

10–17. Check students' work.

Statement: A polygon whose angles have a sum of 180° is a TRIANGLE.

Lesson 8.8

Crossword Puzzle

Across: 4. equal **5.** similar **8.** congruent
10. dilation **11.** grape **12.** unequal
13. equilateral **15.** triangle *MNO*
16. trapezoid
Down: 1. perpendicular **2.** quadrilateral
3. image **6.** irregular **7.** translation
8. congruent **9.** supplementary **14.** addends

Lesson 9.4

Matching Code

1. I **2.** R **3.** R **4.** A **5.** T **6.** I **7.** O
8. N **9.** A **10.** L **11.** N **12.** U **13.** M
14. B **15.** E **16.** R

Statement: If a whole number is not a perfect square, then its square root is an IRRATIONAL NUMBER.

Lesson 9.6

Word Maze

1. Pythagorean **2.** number **3.** real **4.** leg
5. greater **6.** sixty-four **7.** sines
8. *Across:* cosines **8.** *Down:* converse
9. equal **10.** least **11.** tangent **12.** theorem
13. minus **14.** roots **15.** either
16. hypotenuse

Answers to Activities for Substitutes *continued*

Lesson 10.3

Matching Code

1. F **2.** O **3.** R **4.** M **5.** U **6.** L
7. A **8.** S

Statement: To find the area of many plane figures you can use FORMULAS.

Statement: The two bases of a PRISM are congruent polygons. Check students' work.

Lesson 10.7

Hidden Word Puzzle

1. sphere **2.** trapezoid **3.** parallelogram
4. polygon **5.** slant height **6.** surface area
7. edge **8.** prism **9.** cone **10.** cylinder

Statement: A three-dimensional figure with faces that are polygons is a POLYHEDRON.

Statement: The FACES (or BASES) of a cylinder are not polygons. Answers may vary.

Lesson 11.4

Function Flag

1. $y = 10 - x$ or $y = -x + 10$
2. $y = 6 - x$ or $y = -x + 6$
3. $y = 14 - x$ or $y = -x + 14$
4. $y = x + 2$ **5.** $y = x - 2$ **6.** $y = x - 6$
7. $y = x + 6$

8.

9. Check students' work.

Lesson 11.8

Hidden Message

1. linear **2.** input **3.** scatter **4.** relations
5. ordered pair **6.** function **7.** rise **8.** slope
9. output

10. Statement: The Y-INTERCEPT of the line described by $y = 2x + 4$ is 4.

11. Check students' work. **Statement:** The RANGE of a function is the set of all possible output values.

Lesson 12.3

Graphic Message

1. Q **2.** U **3.** A **4.** R **5.** T **6.** I **7.** L
8. E **9. Statement:** The lower QUARTILE is the median of the lower half of an ordered set of data.

Lesson 12.8

Crossword Puzzle

Across:

2. odds **4.** box **5.** dependent
7. permutation **10.** independent
11. stem and leaf **12.** one

Down:

1. combination **3.** complementary
6. quartile **9.** least

Lesson 13.3

Matching Polynomials

1. S **2.** T **3.** A **4.** N **5.** D **6.** A
7. R **8.** D **9.** F **10.** O **11.** R **12.** M

13. Statement: A polynomial is in STANDARD FORM when it is written with the powers of the variables decreasing from left to right.

14. Statement: A BINOMIAL is a polynomial with two terms.

Lesson 13.5

Word Maze

1. monomial **2.** linear **3.** radius
4. simplify **5.** property **6.** regroup
7. *Across:* power **7.** *Down:* product
8. terms **9.** standard **10.** divide
11. expand **12.** squared
13. *Across:* polynomials **13.** *Down:* pairs
14. solution **15.** notation **16.** not

Answers to Activities for Days Before Holidays

Using Integers

1. (top to bottom): 6, 3, 7, 5, 1, 2, 8, 4

2. (top to bottom): 7, 3, 6, 1, 5, 8, 2, 4

3. (top to bottom): 7, 5, 8, 4, 2, 1, 6, 3

4. (top to bottom): 4, 6, 1, 5, 8, 3 2, 7

Multiples Logic

1. A **2.** C **3.** G **4.** B **5.** C **6.** G **7.** B

8. B **9.** B **10.** B **11.** B **12.** F **13.** D

14. E **15.** D **16.** D **17.** B **18.** F **19.** D

20. E **21–27.** Have students justify their choices. **28.** E **29.** B **30.** F

Equations with Fractions *(Sample Answers)*

1. $\frac{1}{4}+\frac{1}{2}$ **2.** $\frac{1}{4}+\frac{2}{3}$ **3.** $\frac{2}{3}+\frac{5}{6}$ **4.** $\frac{2}{3}+\frac{1}{2}$

5. $\frac{1}{8}+\frac{1}{2}+\frac{5}{6}$ **6.** $\frac{5}{6}-\frac{1}{8}$ **7.** $\frac{2}{3}-\frac{1}{4}$ **8.** $\frac{5}{6}-\frac{2}{3}$

9. $\frac{1}{4}\times\frac{1}{8}$ **10.** $\frac{1}{4}\times\frac{1}{2}\times\frac{2}{3}$ **11.** $\frac{2}{5}+\frac{1}{2}$

12. $\frac{3}{8}+\frac{2}{5}$ **13.** $\frac{3}{10}+\frac{2}{5}+\frac{1}{2}$ **14.** $\frac{3}{8}+\frac{1}{2}+\frac{3}{4}$

15. $\frac{3}{4}+\frac{2}{5}-\frac{1}{2}$ **16.** $\frac{1}{2}+\frac{3}{4}-\frac{3}{8}$ **17.** $\frac{2}{5}\times\frac{3}{10}$

18. $\frac{3}{4}\times\frac{1}{2}\times\frac{2}{5}$

Integer Magic Squares

1–4. equations will vary

5. $a = 4$, $b = 1$, $c = 2.5$, $d = 4$, $e = 1.5$

6–9. equations will vary

10. $f = 2$, $g = 4$, $h = 0$, $k = -1$, $m = -2$

11. left to right, top row: $-7, 0, -8$; middle row: $-6, -5, -4$; bottom row: $-2, -10, -3$

12. left to right, top row: $-2, 9, -1$; middle row: 3, 2, 1; bottom row: 5, -5, 6

Sabrina's Fabulous Prices

1. 6 for $1.38 **2.** 4 lb for $3.48

3. 1 lb for $0.43 **4.** 6 for $1.86

5. 5 for $7.55 **6.** 6 lb for $10.20

Using Probability Clues

1. 9 **2.** 4 **3.** 8 **4.** 9 **5.** 6 **6.** 18

Draw the Triangle

1. Possible;

2. Not possible; an equilateral triangle has sides of equal length and interior angles of equal measure (60°).

3. Possible;

4. Possible;

5. Not possible; an equilateral triangle has three 60° angles.

6. Possible;

7. Possible;

8. Possible;

Crack the Code

Crossword Puzzle

Answers to Change of Pace Activities

Lesson 1.2

Number Puzzles (Sample Answers)

2. $3 + 3 + \frac{3}{3}$ **3.** $2 \times (2 + 2 + 2) + \frac{2}{2}$
4. $\frac{4 + 4 + 4}{4}$ **5.** $\frac{5}{5} + \frac{5}{5}$ **6.** $\frac{8 + 8 - 8}{8}$
7. $\frac{6 + 6}{6} + \frac{6}{6}$ **8.** $\frac{7 \times 7}{7} + 7$

Lesson 1.3

Number Patterns (Sample Answers)

1–2. Patterns and expressions will vary.
3. 4 days

Lesson 1.5

Mystery Numbers

Puzzle 1: 22
Puzzle 2: 84
Puzzle 3: Check students' work.

Lesson 1.7

Equation Logic

1. $a = 4$ **2.** $b = 2$ **3.** $c = 12$ **4.** $d = 1$
5. $e = 6$ **6.** $f = 8$

Lesson 2.1

Hidden Message

WYOMING

Lesson 2.3

Integer Squares

1. top row: 4, 3, 2, 1; second row: 3, 2, 1, 0; third row: 2, 1, 0, −1; bottom row: 1, 0, −1, −2
2. top row: −13, −9, −5, −1; second row: −9, −5, −1, 3; third row: −5, −1, 3, 7; bottom row: −1, 3, 7, 11

Lesson 2.5

Means and Integers

1. 81 **2.** 50 **3.** 144 **4.** 29

Lesson 2.7

Properties and Equations

1. circle **2.** circle **3.** rectangle **4.** triangle
5. trapezoid **6.** trapezoid

Lesson 3.2

Guess-and-Check Equations

1. $-6 + (-5)$ **2.** $-3 + (-4)$ **3.** $6 + 3$
4. $4 + (-2)$ **5.** $5 + 2$ **6.** $0 + 1 + (-1)$
or
1. $-6 + (-5)$ **2.** $-4 + (-3)$ **3.** $5 + 4$
4. $3 + (-1)$ **5.** $6 + 1$ **6.** $0 + 2 + (-2)$

Lesson 3.4

Consecutive Integer Puzzles

1. −23, −22 **2.** 23, 24, 25 **3.** −18, −16
4. −32, −30, −28 **5.** −31, −29, −27
6. 6, 7, 8, 9 **7.** −21, −19, −17, −15
8. −2, −1, 0, 1, 2

Lesson 3.5

Area and Perimeter Puzzles

1. C **2.** D **3.** D **4.** F **5.** C **6.** A and E

Lesson 3.7

Balance Scale Puzzle

(1) Weigh any six figurines, three to a pan. If the pans balance, the fake is not among those weighed. Then weigh any two of the three figurines that remain; if these pans balance, the one remaining is the fake. If the pans do not balance, the one in the pan that weighs less is the fake.

(2) If the pans with the three figurines *do not* balance, the fake is on the lighter pan. Then weigh any two of the three figurines on it; if the pans balance, the remaining figurine is the fake.
If they don't balance, the fake is in the lighter pan.

Answers to Change of Pace Activities

Lesson 4.2

Greatest Common Factor

1. 36, 54; 18　**2.** 72, 96; 24

3. $63xy^2$, $126xy^2$; $63xy^2$

Lesson 4.4

Mystery Number

1. 24　**2.** 60　**3.** 2　**4.** 4　**5.** 144　**6.** 4

Lesson 4.5

Forming Equivalent Fractions

1. $\frac{6}{18}, \frac{2}{6}$　**2.** $\frac{3}{6}, \frac{6}{12}$　**3.** $\frac{9}{12}, \frac{12}{16}$

4. $\frac{2}{8}, \frac{8}{32}$　**5.** Sample answers: $\frac{4}{6}, \frac{6}{9}$

Lesson 4.7

Exponents Game

Observe students as they play the game.

Lesson 5.2

Fill in the Fractions

1. $\frac{2}{5} + \frac{1}{2}$　**2.** $\frac{1}{2} + \frac{2}{5} + \frac{3}{10}$　**3.** $\frac{2}{5} + \frac{3}{8}$

4. $\frac{1}{2} + \frac{3}{4} + \frac{3}{8}$　**5.** $\frac{3}{4} + \frac{2}{5} - \frac{1}{2}$

Lesson 5.4

Using Mental Math

Have students explain their strategies.

1. 9　**2.** 9　**3.** -39　**4.** 33　**5.** -25　**6.** 54

7. -54　**8.** 320　**9.** -33

Lesson 5.6

Crack the Code

SNEAKERS

Lesson 5.8

The Mean Variation

1. 12.4　**2.** 15　**3.** $2\frac{2}{3}$　**4.** 100

5. Possible answer: If the mean variation is great, the mean may not be a useful measure of average for that set of data.

Lesson 6.1

Equivalent Equations

(Answers may vary.)

1. $9 + 3n = 15$　**2.** $11 + 2n = 29$

3. $n + (7 + -6) = 4$　**4.** $3n - 5n = 12$

5. $-8 + 4n = 5$

6. $\frac{7(n + 1)}{7} = 14$ or $n + 1 = 14$

Lesson 6.2

Lengths of Segments

1. $AE = 35$, $CD = 39$　**2.** $AE = 24.5$, $EB = 13.5$　**3.** $AE = 9$, $CD = 20$　**4.** $CE = 22$, $ED = 17$　**5.** $AB = 9$, $CE = 2$, $ED = 7$

6. $AE = 1.6$, $EB = 21.6$, $CD = 23.2$

Lesson 6.4

Circles in the Square

1. 1600 square units; 400 square units

2. $16n^2$ square units; $4n^2$ square units

3. 1.5 cm　**4.** 3.5 cm

Lesson 6.6

Triangles and Inequalities

1. $2 < n$　**2.** $0 < 8$　**3.** $2 < 6$　**4.** n is a number greater than 2.　**5.** $x < 8$; $x > -2$; $x > 2$; x is a number greater than 2 and less than 8.

Lesson 7.2

On a Seesaw

1. 240 cm　**2.** 27 kg　**3.** 5 kg

Answers to Change of Pace Activities *continued*

Lesson 7.4

Unreasonable Claims

Explanations will vary; The following statements should be circled: 1, 2, 4, 5, 6, and 8.

Lesson 7.6

Shopping for Rugs

1. $72   **2.** $270   **3.** $445.50   **4.** $80

Lesson 7.7

Describing Probabilities

1. very unlikely   **2.** fifty-fifty   **3.** unlikely
4. very likely   **5.** certain   **6.** impossible

Lesson 8.1

Estimating Angle Measures

Observe students as they play. Ask them to explain how they make their estimates. Guide students to use benchmarks.

Lesson 8.4

Draw the Figure

For Exercises 1–10, check students' drawings.

1. a square   **2.** a quadrilateral with one pair of parallel sides   **3.** a triangle with all sides of different length and each angle less than 90°

4. Not possible; the sum of a triangle's angle measures is 180°.   **5.** a trapezoid with two consecutive right angles or a quadrilateral with two right angles opposite each other.   **6.** an isosceles trapezoid

7. Not possible: a quadrilateral has two diagonals and a pentagon has five; no polygon has three or four.   **8.** a pentagon formed from a square and a triangle that share a side

9. a rectangle or an isosceles trapezoid

10. Not possible: all angles of an equilateral triangle are 60° and thus acute.

Lesson 8.5

Make and Use Equilateral Triangles

Check students' constructions: holes are allowed, but the triangles must be connected along their edges. There are 12 polyiamonds.

Have volunteers draw their polyiamonds on the board.

Lesson 8.6

Symmetrical Letters

Have students share their efforts. Post those words, phrases, and sentences students think are the most creative or funny.

Lesson 9.2

Crack the Code

Answer: TRUMPET

Lesson 9.3

Investigating Triangles

1. A triangle that satisfies the inequality $a^2 + b^2 < c^2$ is an obtuse triangle; the angle opposite leg c must be greater than a right angle.

2. A triangle that satisfies the inequality $a^2 + b^2 > c^2$ is an acute triangle; the angle opposite side c must be smaller than a right angle.

Lesson 9.5

Pythagorean Triples

Students' answers will vary. There are 50 Pythagorean triples with a hypotenuse less than 100, the first few of which, sorted by increasing c, are (3, 4, 5), (6, 8, 10), (5, 12, 13), (9, 12, 15), (8, 15, 17), (12, 16, 20), (15, 20, 25), (7, 24, 25), (10, 24, 26), (20, 21, 29), (18, 24, 30), (16, 30, 34), (21, 28, 35), . . .

Lesson 9.6

Choosing the Right Ratio

Check students' sketches.

1. tan   **2.** cos   **3.** sin

Answers to Change of Pace Activities *continued*

Lesson 10.1

Area of a Rhombus

1. The base and the diagonal $\overline{DB}$ are congruent; the height and the diagonal $\overline{AC}$ are congruent.
2. 6 cm^2 **3.** half the area of the rectangle
4. $A = \frac{1}{2}d_1 d_2$ **5.** 3 cm^2

Lesson 10.3

Word Scramble

1. trapezoid   **2.** diameter   **3.** polyhedron
4. pyramid   **5.** cylinder   **6.** triangular prism
7. cone   **8.** parallelogram

Lesson 10.4

Painting the Pool

1. 219.4 m^2; one method is to find the sum of the areas of the four sides. Two of these sides are congruent, each needing to be first divided into a rectangle and a trapezoid. Then add the area of the two rectangles that form the bottom.
2. 11 cans of paint

Lesson 10.6

Drawing Diagrams

1. 4 cm   **2.** 4 in.   **3.** 2400 m^2 **4.** The box made by cutting 2 inch squares will have the greater volume. First box: $V = 64$ in.^{3}; second box: $V = 72$ in.^{3}; since 72 in.^{3} − 64 in.^{3} = 8 in.^{3}, there is a difference in volume of 8 in.^{3}

Lesson 11.2

When is a Pi Not a Pi?

1.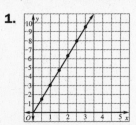

2. Accept answers in the range $C = 3d$ to $C = 3.2d$ **3.** No; because the measurements are all to the nearest quarter inch, there are errors in rounding, which makes the equation of the line slightly different from $C = \pi d$.

Lesson 11.4

The Midpoint Formula

1. $(2, -5)$ **2.** $(-3, -1.5)$ **3.** $(1, -0.5)$
4. $(3, -2)$

Lesson 11.6

Slopes and Squares

1. 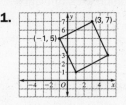   **2.**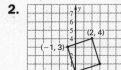

3.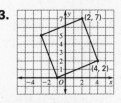

Lesson 11.7

Playing Catch-up

1. Rosa's mother caught up with her at 10 P.M.
2. The table should show how far each travels in an hour until they both have reached a distance of 180 miles.   **3.** The graph should show that the two lines intersect at 10 P.M.

Lesson 12.2

Using a Stem-and-Leaf Plot

Check students' plots to see that they correctly represent the data they have gathered. Challenge: The stem-and-leaf plots will show each piece of data, how the data clusters, and the range of the data. A stem-and-leaf plot is visually effective in that it resembles a bar graph. The box-and-whisker plots will not show all the specific heights, but they will show how the data disperses around the median.

Lesson 12.3

Two Different Impressions

1. Check students' graphs. The graphs should show the same information and should both be correct, but give different impressions of the data.

2. The impressions depend upon whether the vertical scales (wages in dollars) are compressed. For example, a compressed scale with dollar intervals at $0, $10, and $20 will imply slow change in wages. An expanded broken scale (which leaves some of the data values out) with dollar intervals at $0, $10.00, $10.25, $10.50, $10.75, $11.00, $11.25, $11.50, $11.75, $12.00, and $12.25 will imply great increases in wages.

3. Check students' graphs.

Lesson 12.5

Permutations and Combinations

1. They are the same: 10

2. They are the same: 28   **3.** The sum of the numbers of objects taken at a time is equal to the number of objects, i.e., $2 + 3 = 5$, and $2 + 6 = 8$

4. Yes.   **5.** $_{47}C_{45} = {_{47}C_2}$. Since $_{47}C_2 = (47 \times 46) \div (2 \times 1)$, the answer is 1081.

Lesson 12.7

Crack the Code Part 1

CHOCOLATE

Lesson 13.1

Crack the Code Part 2

COFFEEPOT

Lesson 13.4

Problems and Answers

1. $(2x + 1)(x + 5)$; $2x + 11x^2 + 5$

2. $(3y + 2)(y + 8)$; $3y^2 + 26y + 16$

3. $(x^2 + 6x)(4x + 3)$; $4x^3 + 27x^2 + 18x$

4. $(y^2 - 4y)(y^2 + 4)$; $y^5 - 16y$

Lesson 13.5

Is It Magic?

Students' observations and abilities to summarize why the pattern occurs may vary. The product of the first and last terms is 1 less than the square of the middle term. Reasoning: $(x + 1)^2 = x^2 + 2x + 1$; $x(x + 2) = x^2 + 2x$; So, the difference is always 1.

Lesson 13.6

Graph the Path

1. (0, 0)   **2.** (8, 0)   **3.** 2 cm   **4.** 8 cm; check students' graphs.